Are You Normal About
Sex, Love, and Relationships?

Are You Normal About Sex, Love, and Relationships?

Bernice Kanner

St. Martin's Griffin ☎ New York

www.stmartins.com

ISBN 0-312-31107-9

First Edition: February 2004

10 9 8 7 6 5 4 3 2 1

Contents

Introduction

ARE YOU NORMAL ABOUT SEX, LOVE, AND RELATIONSHIPS?
Sex or romance? Women vote for the hug. If the procedure didn't
hurt or cost anything a third of men would have their penises
enlarged. More than half of all women claim they've faked an
orgasm. More than a third of men believe barbecues are a great form
of foreplay and watching football could actually perk up a man's sex
life—providing his team wins.

When it comes to sex and love, how do you fit in? Are you, ahem,
normal? Do you conform to the type, standard, or pattern, the way
most people do?

I've spent more than a year researching how we court and consummate. The giant ad agency Euro RSCG fielded many of my
questions with its international survey, "Love and Lust." The
Chicago-based ad agency Leo Burnett undertook many other parts
of this survey. And I fleshed out the rest with surveys from as far
afield as condom makers, car companies, and health-care providers.

In the bedroom—and wherever else we copulate—we're both
entirely predictable and utterly surprising. Who'd have thought that

almost one in four women would try to conceive without their partners' consent if they wanted a baby; that despite the loudness of the
Moral Majority's cry, 22 percent of women have rented a porn flick
at least once; and that while we talk about equality, more than half
of women (54 percent) say the guy should almost always pay on a
date? Thirty percent insist that even when the woman does the inviting, the man should at least reach for his wallet.

People talk about sex a lot—and worry about it even more. Perhaps finding that others share your insecurities or oddities can make
you feel more at home in this landscape. So pull up a chair and see
how you compare. . . .

1

The Big Picture

IS ALL FAIR IN LOVE AND WAR?
Perhaps because it's been wormed into us as an indisputable truth, four out of five people accept this cliché as the way of the world. But the rest wonder if this isn't really asking whether the end justifies the means.

IS IT MORE IMPORTANT TO FOLLOW YOUR HEAD OR YOUR HEART?
Emotion triumphs over logic. When it comes to choosing a partner, men and women believe that the road to happiness is built more on following their hearts (58 percent) than their heads (41 percent). Sixty-seven percent of women consider themselves romantic, as do the majority of eighteen- to twenty-four-year-olds of both sexes (72 percent vs. 54 percent of those over sixty-five).

WHAT'S THE MOST IMPORTANT QUALITY IN A S.O. (SIGNIFICANT OTHER)?

Doctor, lawyer, Indian chief . . . hardly matters is our belief. For 47 percent, emotional warmth and nurturing are the critical characteristics. For 23 percent, it's a sense of humor. Eighteen percent say their partners must be intelligent and 6 percent say they must have confidence and power. For 4 percent, physical appearance counts the most and 2 percent admit that love can follow money.

DEPENDABILITY OR PASSION?

Eight percent refuse to consider one without the other, insisting that both qualities are essential. But 57 percent say a considerate, dependable partner is more important in the long run than one with an unquenchable zest for life.

WHAT MAKES A MARRIAGE WORK?

A sizzling sex life can cheer you up, but in the the recipe for what makes a good marriage, it's listed very low down, below trust and companionship.

DO YOU BELIEVE THAT MARRIAGE IS A LIFE-LONG COMMITMENT?

It's for keeps. Some 43 percent of women and 45 percent of men—including many who are separated, divorced, or have never been married—believe it should only be ended under extreme circumstances. On the other hand, a fourth of women and 18 percent of men believe people do change and may grow apart over time and that a covenant entered into when they were young shouldn't trap them for life. Roughly a third of both men and women straddle this fence, protesting that people should try hard to save their marriages before divorcing.

WHEN IS THE IDEAL TIME TO MARRY?

It may not be ideal, but it's very real. The average bride nowadays is just over twenty-four and her groom is going on twenty-seven. That's up from the 1980s when the average first-time newlyweds were twenty-two and twenty-six, respectively. This is largely because of a yearning to be financially stable before marrying.

IS IT OKAY FOR MARRIED PEOPLE TO FLIRT?

Theoretically we honor fidelity, but more than half of us (56 percent) don't get our feathers ruffled when our mates strut their stuff. Most feel it adds excitement to a relationship by plucking the jealousy string.

DO YOU THINK MAKING IT HARDER TO DIVORCE WOULD IMPROVE SOCIETY?

Toughening the requirements for divorce would better society, say three out of five people. But only 39 percent strongly support covenant marriages where grounds for divorce are limited to abuse or adultery. At the same time, 47 percent of young men and women say that laws should be changed to make it harder for couples to divorce. Women are likelier than men to believe this.

DO YOU BELIEVE IN THE SEVEN-YEAR ITCH?

Get with the times. The seven-year itch, it appears, is a myth or a relic of slower-paced lives. More divorces happen in the fourth year of marriage than after any other stretch.

DO YOU THINK LOVE IS AS CRITICAL IN MARRIAGE TODAY AS IT ONCE WAS?

Love still makes the world go 'round and plays the same pivotal role in marriages today that it did two decades ago, according to 47 percent of people. A third feel other considerations such as a societal fit or lust have become more important, while 16 percent say the relevance of love has grown on this scale, as women no longer marry just for economic security.

WHO IS MORE ROMANTIC: MEN OR WOMEN?

Women, say 48 percent of us. One in ten choose men, while 39 percent see no gender difference. Men and women split on the issue in like proportions.

DO YOU THINK LIVING TOGETHER BEFORE MARRIAGE BODES WELL?

It may bode well for the individual, but not for the union. Those who adopted the so-called "renter's agreement" are 50 percent likelier to divorce than those who never shared an abode before. They're less committed to weather the tough times.

CAN A COUPLE STAY IN LOVE THROUGH A LONG MARRIAGE?

Although love ebbs and flows, it hovers, say 91 percent of us. Fifty-nine percent believe that sooner or later the desperate passion gives way to a deeper kind of love. But 6 percent feel that after a time boredom erodes love, and then the marriage is pretty dull.

WHO IS MORE SUBMISSIVE IN MOST RELATIONSHIPS?

Perhaps we're just a PC culture, or perhaps equality is still very much a relative term, but 49 percent of us see couplehood as a union of equals. A quarter of people feel women are the more submissive partner and 15 percent see the male as a milquetoast.

HOW MANY PARTNERS IS "NORMAL"?

Any number is "normal" but 17 is the "average" batting average over a lifetime. Some 92 percent of sexually active folks have had ten or more partners in their lifetime. One in ten men and 4 percent of women claim they've had sex with more than 100 partners. Highly educated women seem to have had the most partners, while almost a third of all women have had only one. Closer to home, the "average" American has slept with 14.3 partners—more than the French with 13.2, Australians with 11, and Brits with 8.8 partners. For 45 percent of men and 33 percent of women there haven't been enough notches on their belts.

HAS SEX BECOME TOO SOCIALLY CAVALIER?

It has, if your criteria is knowing all your partners well. Half (51 percent) of people can't recall the first and last name of every person with whom they've slept. The average Joe spends 730 hours a year musing about sex—and 22 hours a year having it. Half of us admit that at least once in our lives we've had sex with someone for whom we had no feelings.

IS SEX OVERRATED?

Compared to work it is, say 62 percent of people. Only 20 percent of men say they have sex as a way to unwind after a tough day. Fifty-two percent would rather play soccer or go to the gym. Eleven percent can even imagine going through life without ever experiencing sex—and not regretting it.

HOW ABOUT FALLING IN LOVE?
Over the course of a lifetime, we fall in love, on average, six times—starting with puppy love at thirteen and then the first serious relationship four years later. One out of four of us falls in love at least ten times, with women prone to more episodes than men. In a lifetime, 12 percent of us have had at least three unrequited loves.

DO YOU THINK THERE'S ONLY ONE PERSON OUT THERE FOR YOU?
Nearly three out of four Americans believe there is "one true love" out there to fulfill their destiny. This belief is strongest among those married a long time, (79 percent), very recently (76 percent), or the poor.

DOES ABSENCE MAKE THE HEART GROW FONDER?
Two-thirds of us (69 percent) think separation fans the flames but 31 percent figure out of sight, out of mind. Statistically, long distance relationships fail three hundred times more often than those couples who see each other daily or even weekly.

IF LOVE HAS FLED, SHOULD THE PAIR PART AND START NEW LIVES?
Once again it's a cultural divide. Just over a third of Americans (35 percent) believe that if the marriage has gone asunder for lack of love, it's best to seek amour elsewhere. In contrast, 78 percent of Brazilians feel that way. The English, Indians, and Chinese are somewhere in the middle, averaging about 46 percent.

THINK SEXUAL EQUALITY HAS DAMPENED ROMANCE?
Nearly half of us (49 percent) feel the movement toward equal rights and opportunities for women has thrown cold water on romance. Thirteen percent feel it has stimulated arousal. Even the gloomiest, however, think romance is still rampant, feminism or not.

CAN WE HELP WHO WE FALL IN LOVE WITH?

Sixty-three percent of us say "you betcha," and that you can direct and govern who you fall for.

DO YOU THINK GREAT SEX CAN TRIGGER LOVE?

Men and women think differently here. Sixty-nine percent of women say if they didn't love their partner before sex, no matter how great it was, they won't love him after. But 46 percent of men say a magic sexual experience can induce emotional feelings that weren't apparent before—that people's behavior during sex says a lot about their character that would make them appealing, or disturbing. Indeed, 40 percent of men and 35 percent of women believe that great sex with their partners was instrumental in triggering the relationship.

DO THE WORDS "NICE" OR "SWEET" TURN YOU OFF?

Nice and sweet are not the words we want to hear. More than two times as many people (41 percent vs. 16 percent) translate them as "boring" and "wimpy" and dial down the subject's sexual allure. The rest view the words as neutral.

HOW MUCH DOES FALLING IN LOVE AFFECT HAPPINESS?

Big surprise: it does a lot more for men than women. One in five men compared to just 14 percent of women list falling in love as a key factor affecting their happiness levels, according to Thomson Holidays. For women, spending time with friends is higher up the happiness chart.

IF A RELATIONSHIP NEEDS WORK, IS IT WORTH THE EFFORT?

That depends on what kind of relationship it is . . . and what they will get out of it . . . and what they have already invested in it and gotten out of it . . . and what it will cost them to work on it. If there's a lot of emotional capital on the table, 81 percent of women and 89 percent of men think it justifies investing more. The rest feel that if it's broken, best to throw it away, without tossing good money after bad.

IS LOVE BLIND?

Most people—especially younger folks—certainly believe that some things in life simply can't be understood and who we love and why are two of them. But older people with more life experience say that love is eyes wide open, appreciating and recognizing who the other person is and what the attraction is.

WHAT CONSTITUTES SEX AND WHAT'S JUST FOOLIN' AROUND?

Blame it on the Bill Clinton–Monica Lewinsky scandal for introducing the "just foolin' " concept into the mainstream. Technically "sex" refers to stimulation of sex organs, but most people talk about it to mean only intercourse. More than one in ten high school students who called themselves virgins admitted they'd had oral sex and more than one in three had petted heavily or had "outercourse." Seventy percent of the boys had gone down on girls and 57 percent of the girls had performed fellatio at least once before they had "sex."

WHICH CARRIES MORE WEIGHT: FIREWORKS OR FRIENDSHIP?

More than two out of three say that the excitement fizzles but the qualities that establish a friendship grow in a romance.

WHAT'S MOST SOUGHT AFTER: MODEST OR MOSTEST?

That depends on whether the seeker is inner or outer directed. Extroverts tend to look for busty, nude *Playboy* models, while introverts, overwhelmed by the flash, incline toward less busty, fully-dressed, pale, thin English-rose types.

HAVE MEN BECOME TOO SOFT AND SENSITIVE?

They've still got a ways to go before that becomes a problem, say 73 percent of women.

IS A ROMANTIC CHASE AND CHALLENGE STILL EXCITING?

Even in an age of sexual equality, 60 percent of both men and women confess that the idea of a sexual chase is more of a turn-on than equal willingness on both sides.

DID YOU WATCH *JOE MILLIONAIRE* PICK ZORA?

Drawn by the question whether it was money or love, 40 million viewers watched the romantic payoff of the reality dating drama—as Evan Marriott admitted to Zora that he wasn't rich.

FOR A WOMAN, WHO SHOULD COME FIRST, HUSBAND OR KIDS?

Twice as many say the marriage is more important than its progeny (13 percent vs. 6 percent). But 72 percent insist that husband, children, and self are all equally important.

SHOULD COHABITANTS GET THE SAME BENEFITS AS MARRIEDS?

Nearly half of us—45 percent—feel the government should provide cohabiting and same-sex couples with the same benefits—and tax penalties—as married couples.

IS IT OKAY FOR A WOMAN TO HAVE A CHILD ON HER OWN?

A majority of people (62 percent) think that while it's far from ideal, it's all right for an unwed adult woman to have a child on her own.

IS MARRIAGE AN ANTIQUATED CONCEPT?

The knot may have its faults, but for 88 percent of us, marriage is still relevant and the best system that we've got or can envision.

2

State of Your Union

DO YOU EXPECT YOUR SPOUSE TO BE YOUR SOUL MATE?
If you've never been married and are young, chances are you do. Ninety-four percent of teens and Gen Xers anticipate that their spouse will be the yin to their yang. Older folks take into account that marriage may also be an economic, logistics, and parenthood partnership.

ARE YOU AFRAID OF COMMITMENT?
Thirty-seven percent of women and 17 percent of men confess that the fear of commitment is why they call their significant other, their "semi" significant other.

DO YOU FEAR BEING ON YOUR OWN?
Twenty-nine percent of people are sufficiently unsettled by the prospect of being by themselves that they stay in relationships that may not scratch their every itch. But almost half say they are not at all afraid to be on their own.

WHAT'S MOST ENDEARING ABOUT YOUR SPOUSE? MOST IRRITATING?

For a third of us hearing him or her murmur "I love you" every day is worth the price of admission. On the other hand, a third find their partners' propensity to not listen to be most infuriating. And 18 percent of women and 13 percent of men hate their partners' cooking. Fifty-seven percent of us say having a resident best friend is the nicest part of being married. Four percent take a less chivalrous—or more practical—stance, claiming they can get sex whenever they want.

WHAT'S THE NICEST PART OF MARRIED SEX?

Its intimacy, say 58 percent of men and women. Another 22 percent claim that marriage has freed them of inhibitions, making their sex hot and explosive. Twelve percent are enraptured by the coziness.

DO YOU ALWAYS CONSULT WITH YOUR SPOUSE BEFORE BUYING SOMETHING BIG?

"Big" is the operative word here. For the most part, couples say they seek consensus on purchases that cost an average of $134. But 62 percent buy their own clothes without consulting their S.O. regardless of the price and just over half purchase jewelry for themselves without prior (or subsequent) approval.

WHO IS MOST LIKELY TO INITIATE A "RELATIONSHIP" DISCUSSION?

Eighty-three percent of women say they are the ones most likely to begin the discussion that starts with "Let's talk about us . . ." Only 57 percent of men, though, agree that it's the women who speak first.

WHAT DO YOU MOST WANT FROM YOUR WIFE THAT YOU'RE NOT GETTING?

We know that women want to be listened to, but what men want has always been something of a mystery. Mystery solved: 38 percent of men want their women to show them more affection and 30 percent want their spouses to be more open spiritually. Twenty-six percent of men and women wish their partners would ask them more about themselves and their day.

HAVE YOU EVER WISHED TO WAKE UP IN THE MORNING AND SUDDENLY BE SINGLE?

A third of women said they thought about getting the whole bed for themselves, while just one in four suppose their husbands had ever considered seeking a divorce. Almost four out of every five couples who have been miserable at one point in their marriage but didn't follow through on their impulses to divorce found themselves happy five years later after sticking it out. Researchers have dubbed this the "marital endurance ethic."

HOW OFTEN DO YOU AND YOUR PARTNER FIGHT?

First let's define terms: an argument is not a fight. A fight is when you call in the artillery and aim to flatten your partner emotionally. This, it seems, we're not doing all that much. Sixty-two percent of women and 43 percent of men say they hardly ever go at it with each other and 22 percent of men and 16 percent of women say they do so perhaps once a month. One in five men and 15 percent of women guestimate that they brawl once a week and 15 percent of men and 6 percent of women say they wrangle more often. Then again, some researchers suggest that bickering may actually be the key to marital bliss and preferable to sweeping problems under the rug.

DOES YOUR RELATIONSHIP MAKE YOU FEEL SECURE? CONFIDENT?

An overwhelming majority (90 percent) say one of the best perks of their relationships is the sense of comfort and security they provide. Eighty-three percent feel considerably more confident in themselves since hitching up with their partners.

DOES BEING MARRIED MAKE YOU FEEL SEXIER?

Plighting your troth may make you feel hot. Sixty-nine percent of marrieds say they feel sexier being part of a married couple than they did before they walked down the aisle. It may be more than a feeling; two-thirds of newly marrieds claim they do it more than when they were single, with half having sex two or three times a week and 14 percent, daily. And 63 percent say they're likelier to have surprise quickies than before they wed. Single men average twenty-one minutes per session; marrieds fourteen minutes. For 82 percent the sex has improved, largely because they're sharing so much outside the bedroom.

IF YOU HAD THE CHANCE TO DO IT ALL AGAIN, WOULD YOU?
Despite what the divorce tally reveals, 93 percent of married people say they would gladly walk down the aisle with their current spouse if they knew what their future held.

DO YOU TRUST YOUR PARTNER ALL THE TIME?
Eight in ten happily marrieds say they have no doubts about their partners. That doesn't mean they'll never hear a lie from their partner, however.

COULD YOU LIVE WITHOUT YOUR MATE?
Seventy percent of women believe they could—and just might have to someday. But 38 percent don't think their husband could live without them.

DO YOU ENJOY CARING FOR YOUR S.O. WHEN HE OR SHE IS SICK?
There's a reason the marriage vow says "in sickness and in health." Some 54 percent of women and 52 percent of men say taking care of an ill partner is one of the aspects of intimacy they find most rewarding.

HAVE YOU BEEN SERVED BREAKFAST IN BED RECENTLY?
Fewer than a third of us have been served breakfast in bed in the past year, although virtually everyone who has been remembers it. At the same time, 84 percent of women say they remember the last time they received flowers, and even the conversation surrounding it.

IN YOUR RELATIONSHIP, WHO SPENDS MORE ON HIM- OR HERSELF?
Forty-four percent of couples say the woman does and 37 percent point to the man. Eighteen percent claim that neither is more high maintenance than the other.

IN YOUR RELATIONSHIP, WHO WANTS TO TALK MORE?

Fifty-nine percent of couples say the woman is more talkative, while 20 percent point to the man. Nineteen percent claim that neither is loquacious.

DO YOU STEAL THE COVERS OR ARE THEY STOLEN FROM YOU?

Three-fourths of us—men and women alike—accuse our mates of hogging the covers. For women that's a cardinal offense because 83 percent use a cover more for the weight or security it confers than for the warmth.

DOES YOUR GUY LEAVE THE TOILET SEAT UP AFTER USING IT?

Women invariably say they find it up but 46.5 percent of men in America insist they always put the seat down after they use it.

HAS YOUR RELATIONSHIP BECOME TOO COMFORTABLE?

A third of women and one in five men feel that their partners take them for granted. Most like the level of comfort that allows them to feel totally relaxed with their partner. Forty-three percent of women and 55 percent of men say they are so relaxed with their mate that even passing gas in front of their partner is forgivable and no cause for anxiety. After delivering his baby, a little gas while sitting on the couch doesn't constitute a breach of code.

DO YOU WEAR EACH OTHER'S CLOTHES?

Consider it a degree of comfort: 56 percent of women and 16 percent of men routinely plunder their partners' closets for wardrobe.

DO YOU HAVE YOUR OWN SIDE OF THE BED?

Four out of five women and three out of four men say they wouldn't be caught dead sleeping on the "wrong" side of the bed—even when they stay in hotels or at friends' houses, and even if it means limited access to the duvet.

HOW SATISFIED ARE YOU IN YOUR CURRENT RELATIONSHIP WITH RESPECT TO SEX?

Just 16 percent of lovers think that what they've got is as good as it gets. Another 21 percent think that theirs is better than most, while 12 percent figure their sex life is about average. One in five feels it's simply got to get better.

WAS SEX WITH YOUR HUSBAND OR WIFE THE BEST YOU'VE EXPERIENCED?

Two-thirds of married women feel that sex with their husbands was the best they ever experienced. For 13 percent, it was when they were single and for 9 percent, during an affair.

HOW SATISFIED ARE YOU IN YOUR RELATIONSHIP WITH RESPECT TO COMMUNICATION?

Forty-seven percent of us think that on this front our relationship is head and shoulders above the norm. Nineteen percent admit they've got a ways to go in talking with each other. At the same time, more than half of us (51 percent) think we share a closer intimacy than most people do. Only 22 percent regard their relationship as insufficiently intimate.

HOW INDEPENDENT ARE YOU IN YOUR CURRENT RELATIONSHIP?

Seventeen percent of those in relationships find them smothering, depriving them of the essential freedoms they need. Even people deeply in love (45 percent of women and 42 percent of men) would welcome a vacation without their S.O.

DO YOUR FRIENDS PREFER WHEN YOU LEAVE YOUR MATE HOME WHEN YOU GO TO A PARTY?

Amazingly, 28 percent of women and men say they're much more welcome as a solo than as part of a pair.

DO YOU AND YOUR PARTNER SHARE MANY MUTUAL INTERESTS?

Twice as many people are dissatisfied with the amount of mutual interests they and their partner share than are exuberant or even content about this.

FEEL THERE'S OPPORTUNITY TO PERSONALLY GROW AND DEVELOP IN YOUR RELATIONSHIP?

Thirty-nine percent think their relationship affords ample opportunity to spread their wings but an almost equal number (36 percent) feel hog-tied to some degree.

HOW DEPENDENT ARE YOU ON YOUR SIGNIFICANT OTHER FOR YOUR HAPPINESS?

Not very, say 55 percent. Just 8 percent think their world is largely wrapped up in their mate.

IF YOU EVER SPLIT UP, WHAT WOULD CAUSE IT?

The most common reasons women give for leaving husbands is mental cruelty and neglect. When they state legal grounds for divorce, about half report they have been emotionally abused, not by their husbands' overt efforts to drive them crazy but by their indifference, failure to communicate, and emotional and physical abandonment. Few divorces occur because of physical abuse, infidelity, alcoholism, criminal behavior, fraud, or other serious grounds.

WOULD YOU EVER TRADE IN YOUR ENGAGEMENT RING FOR A BIGGER, BETTER DIAMOND?

Fifty-four percent of women recoiled at the suggestion when Diamond Cutters International asked them in 1988. Fifteen years later, 81 percent of the 46 percent who would have traded their rings were divorced, suggesting they were interested in upgrading other things, too.

HAVE YOU CHANGED WHO YOU ARE TO GET THE APPROVAL OF YOUR PARTNER?

Fifty-eight percent of people in relationships concede that they have become neater, more goal-oriented, less of a procrastinator, less of a couch potato, or in some other way changed to curry favor from a lover.

WOULD YOU POSTPONE OR GIVE UP YOUR CAREER TO RAISE A FAMILY?

Eighty-nine percent of women who want children would put off working to raise their kids—although 63 percent say they'd only do it for a year or two. Nine percent wouldn't take the time off at all and 2 percent say they would make that sacrifice, but very reluctantly.

WOULD YOU MARRY SOMEONE WITH THE RIGHT QUALITIES WHOM YOU DIDN'T LOVE?

In this country, 86 percent of us say a resounding "no." But in nations where arranged marriages are more the norm, only 24 percent would not consider it.

HOW LONG COULD YOU ABSTAIN FROM SEX OR MASTURBATION?

Seven percent say they could make it through a day but not much more and one in four claim they can go without for several days. Twenty-eight percent say they'd be perfectly comfortably abstaining for more than a week, while for 19 percent, going for more than a month would pose no hardship. At the other end, 7 percent say they could lay off for half a year and 4 percent could hold out for a year. Another 7 percent could go without sex indefinitely.

IF AN ACCIDENT LEFT YOUR FIANCÉ A PARAPLEGIC, WOULD YOU STILL MARRY?

Two-thirds of people (68 percent) think they would go through with the wedding as planned. The rest feel that the whole ballpark has changed before the "in-sickness-and-in-health" bonds locked them in.

IS YOUR MATE TOO JEALOUS?

More than six out of ten men and women believe that their partner is just where he or she should be when it comes to jealousy—protective and interested enough, but not cloyingly covetous. Those who believe their partner is too jealous are likeliest to live in Turkey (40 percent), Portugal (36 percent), Poland (31 percent), Spain (30 percent), or Greece (25 percent).

DO YOU REACH OUT AND TOUCH SOMEONE?

Two-thirds of both husbands and wives (69 percent) have called each other just to say "I love you." Some 31 percent of both sexes say they never have. Three out of five of us say we've left love notes where our mates can come upon them.

DO YOU SAY I LOVE YOU WHEN HANGING UP THE PHONE?

Seventy percent of couples routinely say the magic words just before hanging up and 65 percent do so when they meet and part. Fifty-five percent speaketh thus during sex and 37 percent utter it randomly.

COMMUNICATE WITH YOUR SIGNIFICANT OTHER DURING THE DAY?

Thanks to mobile phones, couples touch base very often, it seems. One in three contact each other more than ten times in a day. Four our of five connect to say they're running late, while two out of three ask them to do something they had forgotten. Forty-two percent buzz to check whether they need anything from the shops, and 28 percent to find out what's for dinner. One in twenty have even called their partner from the doorstep to let them know they are home.

WOULD THE LOTTERY CHANGE YOUR RELATIONSHIP?

Winning the $10-million jackpot would juice up a lot of flagging relationships. Three out of four promise they'd spend more time with their partners and 16 percent say they'd get married. On the other hand, 7 percent view this as a get out of jail card, figuring they'd spend less time with their partners, and 3 percent say they'd get a divorce.

3

Body Works

✗ HAVE YOU EVER MEASURED YOUR PENIS?

More than four out of five guys admit they've taken a ruler to their member. They must have been shocked by what they found. Men say the average erect penis is ten inches (women guesstimate four inches) but medical researchers say a flaccid one falls (or stands) somewhere between three to four inches and five to seven inches when erect. The average one at attention is 5.877 inches, about the size of a medium cup of coffee at Starbucks. Almost half of men and women (46.8 percent) claim size doesn't matter. A third of men (33.8 percent) have a crooked or curved penis.

✗ AND YOUR TESTICLES?

Probably when you had the tape measure out it was a twofer. The average testicle is two inches long and an inch wide, mushrooming by 50 percent when ready for action. Call it left-balled, but more than 56 percent of men hang left, meaning their left-sided testicle hangs lower than the right. In 21 percent of men, it's the right ball that droops. That means fewer than one in four men are more or less equally hung.

DO YOU NEED AN EXTRA-LARGE CONDOM?

Lots of men think they do—or wish it were so—but in reality only 7.3 million males (about 6 percent) could actually fill an extra-large condom. Some 16.5 percent of men consider themselves well endowed, while 71 percent judge themselves to be average sized and 12.4 percent suspect they're on the small side.

ARE YOU CIRCUMCISED?

Nine out of ten older men in this country have had fifteen square inches of nerve-rich erogenous tissue snipped away (mainly at birth, although less than one percent have undertaken this extreme act as adults). But nowadays, just over 60 percent of all baby boys born in America have their foreskins removed. Those born in the Northeast and Midwest are more likely to go under the knife than westerners.

HOW OFTEN DO YOU GET BLUEBALLS?

You know that slightly achy feeling in the testes that occurs when you get an erection but don't ejaculate? It doesn't happen every time the urge is there, but the discomfort, which evaporates quickly, happens frequently.

WHAT'S YOUR SPERM COUNT?

If only your total net worth were this high! During orgasm the normal guy emits 120 million to 600 million sperm. (Only about four hundred of them will get anywhere *near* the egg.) Since 1940, the average male's sperm count has dropped 42 percent, from 113 million per milliliter to 66 million. Eighteen-year-olds have an average 30 percent more sperm than 45-year-olds. Ejaculate contains, on average, a teaspoon of protein-rich semen at only five calories (dieters must come up with other excuses for not swallowing). It shoots out at twenty-eight miles an hour before it enters Earth's atmosphere, so to speak, and then abruptly and sharply slows down.

LADIES?

The average vagina is three to four inches long and expands during penetration. And the average clitoris is sixteen millimeters long although packed with eight thousand nerve fibers, twice as many as the penis.

ARE YOU IN TIP-TOP FORM?

Fifty-six percent of men say they're functioning at their biological peak.

ARE YOU UP ON BIOLOGY?

Eighty-three percent of men over fifty know the function of a woman's ovaries, but only 42 percent know the function of their own prostate gland, according to the American Foundation for Urologic Disease.

ARE YOU TOTALLY HAPPY WITH YOUR BODY?

Only one in one hundred of us are. And just 7 percent are content with their image. Ninety-three percent say they're working to better their face or body. Sixty-one percent are unhappy with their stomach flab and almost as many are dismayed by their bottoms, thighs, and hips. Surprisingly, 30 percent more women are worried about their arms than their breast size.

HOW OFTEN DO YOU THINK ABOUT YOUR SIZE OR SHAPE?

Seventy-eight percent of us think about it—or more accurately torture ourselves with it—every day. Sixty-eight percent of us think we'd be a lot happier if our bodies only cooperated.

HOW FAR ARE YOU PREPARED TO GO FOR IT?

One in ten women have taken drugs in their quest to obtain corporeal perfection and two-thirds have already undergone or would consider undergoing plastic surgery. The most popular procedures: liposuction and tummy tucks.

IF IT DIDN'T HURT OR COST ANYTHING, WOULD YOU HAVE YOUR PENIS ENLARGED?

A third of men admit that they would clamber onto the operating table.

SAME CONDITIONS AS ABOVE, LADIES, WOULD YOU CHANGE THE SIZE OF YOUR BREASTS?

Only 6 percent of women say they'd consider breast surgery (5 percent to augment and 1 percent to diminish) if it were pain- and monetarily free.

IS YOUR GUY GROWING BREASTS?

Sorry to say that this condition, called gynecomastia, occurs in 40 percent of men. And 1 percent of breast cancers occur in men.

DO YOU HAVE MORE THAN TWO NIPPLES OR INVERTED ONES?

Anne Boleyn was said to have six nipples and she still became a (short-lived) queen. One in five hundred women have more than the customary two nipples and one in ten women have inverted nipples. Many women have hair around their nipples.

WHEN YOU LOOK AT YOUR CHEST, DO YOU LIKE WHAT YOU SEE?

Only one in ten young women like the size and shape of their breasts. The two breasts are often slightly different in size—just like people's hands and feet.

WHAT'S YOUR BRA SIZE?

In the last decade the average bra size has ballooned from a 34B to a 36B. In the next few years it's predicted the average bra size will be 36C or 36D. The average woman's bustline is 35.9 inches. Fifteen percent of women wear an A cup and 44 percent a B. Twenty-eight percent buy a C cup and 10 percent a D. Just 3 percent wear something else, such as AA or DD. When aroused, breasts swell up as much as 25 percent.

WHAT SIZE BREASTS DO YOU PREFER?

While men may like to fantasize about big boobs or elbow each other about them, 81 percent say they'd prefer medium-size ones if they were women and 53 percent actually prefer medium-size ones on their women. Five percent even like their women to have small breasts. Only 14 percent say bigger is better, while 28 percent say any size is fine.

ARE BREAST IMPLANTS SATISFYING?

Forty-seven percent of men think women look sexier before they have breast implants compared to 21 percent who find the postoperative look more seductive.

GUYS, WHAT'S YOUR FAVORITE PART OF A WOMAN'S BODY?

Not surprisingly considering their conditioning, 31 percent of men admit it's the breast. But somewhat surprisingly, even more (43 percent) view legs as their favorite and most authentic aspect of a woman's body. Another 26 percent find the small of a woman's back most alluring.

HOW ABOUT HER FACE?

The eyes have it. Two-thirds of men are drawn here, whereas 24 percent are drawn to women's hair and 8 percent to their lips and smiles.

IS PENIS ENVY REAL?

Having a penis can be a hoot. It hangs out, and doesn't hide inside the body. It's easy to play with and it even allows its owners to pee standing up. But that doesn't mean it's on women's wish lists. Freud would have us believe that women are pining away for a penis, but given the choice, only one in five would opt for one.

4

The Dating Game

A successful man is one who makes more money than his woman can spend. A successful woman is one who can find such a man. That's one goal of dating. What's yours?

WHEN YOU THINK OF "DATING," WHAT COMES TO MIND?
For men, it's sex, sex, followed by more sex, women, and then fun. For women it's fun. Despite that, for both men and women, dating is more a means to an end than the end itself. For 42 percent of men and 51 percent of women the main objective is to establish a relationship; only 33 percent of men and 29 percent of women say the goal is only to have a good time.

ARE YOU FRIGHTENED OF COMMITMENT?
Some women are, but commitment-phobia is much more a guy thing. Almost half (49 percent) of single men say they're not actively seeking a partner. Fifty-one percent of women think that most men fear commitment and 55 percent believe that men are not monogamous by nature. Fifteen percent of men confess they'd dread the loss

of their freedom, while another 15 percent panic about the responsibility of a family. One in ten thinks someone better might come along.

ARE YOU MORE ATTRACTED TO SOMEONE LIKE YOU OR VERY DIFFERENT THAN YOU?

It's true that opposites attract, but not as much as similar types do. Fifty-seven percent of both men and women say they're more likely to go for someone who is very much like them, rather than someone who is very different. And 57 percent of women claim they don't tend to date men who remind them of their dads.

WHAT WOULD A PERFECT DATE LOOK LIKE?

Forget tall, dark, and handsome. The perfect male is of average height, with blue eyes and short, neat brown hair. He's got a narrow waist and broad shoulders—qualities consistent with strength and the ability to earn a living. The ideal woman is also of average height, with blue eyes, full lips and wavy, shoulder-length brown hair.

WHAT WOULD MAKE FOR A ROMANTIC DATE?

A secluded spot would do the trick for 81 percent, while 12 percent would prefer to nuzzle over dinner and dancing. Seven percent would rather go to a movie and have a late drink.

HOW DID YOU MEET YOUR CURRENT BEAU?

The blind date still looks pretty good as a portal to romance. Forty percent of women and 34 percent of men in happy relationships say they'd been fixed up by friends. That ties the day-to-day environment of office or school as prowling grounds for guys but handily surpasses those venues for women (26 percent). Parties also pay off: 17 percent of men and 11 percent of women say they met their other half at a jamboree. Slightly more than one in eight recent relationships started online and 9 percent of women and 2 percent of men say they connected at a bar or club.

HAVE YOU EVER BEEN ON A BLIND DATE?

Nearly two out of every five adults have and 36 percent of those who never did would like to. For two out of three (69 percent), friends did the fixing up, while 11 percent have to thank (or blame) a coworker. Sixteen percent credit a brother, sister, or some other relative but not parents—they account for just 1 percent of matchups.

WHERE WOULD YOU LOOK FOR FUTURE DATES?

Two out of three of us say they'd ask friends, coworkers, or family who they know. Others would scour their workmates (36 percent); schoolmates (27 percent); online chat mates (26 percent); and who's hanging at the bars or coffee shops (26 percent). Fewer than one in five singles meet at church (or some place like it), the supermarket, library, or bookstore. Divorcées and widows are far likelier to reconnect on the Internet than anywhere else. Another big potential is a chance encounter: some 31 percent of men and 27 percent of women found a New Year's kiss with a stranger initiated a steamy new romance.

IS THE GYM JUST FOR WORKING OUT?

It's just as much for working in . . . into a relationship. Two out of three of us (69 percent) think the gym is a great place to meet potential date prospects, an added boon to shaping up.

WHEN YOU GO TO A BAR OR CLUB, DO YOU USUALLY GO ALONE?

Men say sure, but three out of five women would not venture into a bar or club by themselves. Perhaps they should. Half of nightclub goers have had a serious relationship with someone they met in a bar. Four percent even married that pickup.

HAVE YOU EVER RUN A PERSONAL AD?

Half of single men looking for love have placed ads—and responded to others. But only one in five women has ever run an ad. Women are far likelier to respond to others' ads: 38 percent have gotten back to people whose ads provoked them.

DID YOUR AD MENTION CHILDREN? WEIGHT? ASK FOR A PHOTO?

A third of women mention children in their ads, compared with just 8 percent of men. Nearly three out of four men mention their weight in a personal ad, compared with 43 percent of women. And it seems men are more concerned with appearances: 40 percent of their ads ask for a photo, compared with 15 percent of women's ads.

WHAT DO YOU THINK ABOUT DATING AGENCIES AS A WAY TO CONNECT?

Fifty-seven percent of those in the market disdain dating agencies as a good way to connect.

WOULD YOU TRUST YOUR MOM TO SET YOU UP ON A DATE?

Compared to Mom, the agencies may not be such a bad idea after all. Seventy-four percent of men claim they'd never trust their mothers to get involved here.

WHAT DO YOU THINK OF SPEED DATING?

With one-minute managers and six-minute abs, why not three-minute dates? Collectively we're evenly split with 48 percent considering this an efficient way to meet people, and 51 percent turning their noses up at this musical chairs for grown-ups because you can't make a smart decision in a nanosecond. In an average night, you can go on about forty dates and most people make an average of six matches. Most people do it with a friend.

HOW DO YOU LET SOMEONE KNOW YOU WANT THEM TO ASK YOU OUT?

Flattery will get you there: 51 percent say they pay extra attention when the object of their interest talks or laughs. One in four touches the person a lot and 23 percent send the word out through a friend.

DO YOU HAVE SOME SORT OF FIRST-DATE RITUAL?

Pull on the lucky boxers or spiffy Manolo Blahniks. Layer on a shade of your favorite opalescent nail color. Quaff a glass of milk half an hour before the date arrives. Call your best chum exactly twenty-seven minutes before you set out. Nearly *everyone* has some sort of first-date ritual to make them feel more comfortable and confident.

✗ DO YOU BELIEVE IN THE "WHERE IS OUR RELATIONSHIP GOING" TALK?

Not a peep of it, say one in four people who think a relationship should take its course without the conversation. Another 10 percent grudgingly admit that maybe a year of exclusive dating means it's okay for the chat. On the other hand, 23 percent say talk it out by the eighth date and another 23 percent opt for an assessment after roughly three months. Twelve percent say six months is a good time to take stock and another 3 percent say they wait until eight months have passed before acknowledging something is going on.

HOW SOON DO YOU DECIDE TO JUST DATE EACH OTHER?

Eight percent claim to know from the first date that it's exclusive, while 18 percent claim that after the first few weeks, unspoken, it just happens. For 14 percent it becomes restricted to just each other once sex has entered the picture. Eleven percent say it naturally evolves after a few months, whereas 43 percent say it only happens after a discussion and mutual decision. Two percent claim they don't believe in exclusive relationships.

✗ HOW LONG DO YOU TAKE TO DECIDE IF SOMEONE IS WORTH DATING A SECOND TIME?

Much less time for the guy than for the gal. It takes an average of one hour for a women to decide if a man is worth dating a second time. It only takes a man fifteen minutes to decide about the woman.

✗ HAVE YOU EVER TRIED TO CONNECT ONLINE?

Twenty-nine percent of college kids claim they've met some great people here but 18 percent don't trust the Net as a viable way to connect. One in six of us has asked for a date via email. A third of those in the market admit they've had a strictly cyber relationship with someone they've never physically met.

DO YOU VISIT ONE SITE OR PLAY THE ONLINE FIELD?

Nearly 53 percent of visitors to personals sites bet their prospects for love exclusively on one site, 30 percent use two or three sites, and 17 percent visit four or more. While women make up a slight majority of those online, men account for 54 percent of those visiting personals sites.

HOW LONG AFTER A FIRST DATE DO YOU USUALLY WAIT TO CALL?

More than three out of five guys (62 percent) wait just a day or two if they're keen on advancing the cause. But 26 percent wait for three to five days and 1.6 percent for a week or two. Eight percent claim they wait for the girl to call.

IF SOMEONE YOU DIDN'T LIKE ASKED FOR YOUR PHONE NUMBER, WOULD YOU GIVE IT?

Half of men say sure but more than three out of four women take pains to nip something unpleasant in the bud; they either give out a wrong number or decline to give one out at all.

WHEN YOU FIRST BEGAN DATING, HOW OFTEN DID YOU USUALLY SEE EACH OTHER?

Just 24 percent of women and 14 percent of men say it usually starts out slow and measured. But 39 percent of women and 58 percent of men say when they fall, they fall hard; from the start they began to see each other three or more times a week.

AT WHAT AGE WOULD YOU LET YOUR KIDS GO OUT ON A DATE?

Sixteen seems to be the magic moment; 41 percent of parents consider that the firing gun. Twenty-one percent are more liberal, condoning it as early as thirteen or fourteen. Nineteen percent think the right age to begin is 17.

AS A KID DID YOU EVER SNEAK OUT OF THE HOUSE TO GO ON A DATE?

One in five of us recall resorting to this to circumvent parental controls.

WHAT DO YOU "EXPECT" ON A FIRST DATE?

Thirty-nine percent of men expect nothing more than a kiss—if there's mutual attraction. But assuming the get-together was a hit, 39 percent of people would like to end it with a French kiss, 19 percent with a kiss on the cheek, and 17 percent with a hug. Four percent think a handshake is all you should offer. The rest would go for greater shades of intimacy.

ON WHAT DATE DO YOU USUALLY DO THE DEED?

Nine percent say they go right at it, while one in five rein themselves in until the second or third date. A third wait a few weeks and 37 percent say they hold off until they've been dating a few months. Forty-something women jump into bed quicker with a new partner than women in their twenties; 46 percent have sex within five dates versus 34 percent of Gen Xers.

AT WHAT POINT DID YOU SHARE KEYS?

Of those who live together, half waited until six months of intense dating and half waited for at least a year before sharing a place.

HOW LONG SHOULD YOU DATE BEFORE GETTING MARRIED?

You can still believe in love at first sight, but don't you want to make sure? Just one in five of us (21 percent of men and 19 percent of women) say they'd know if they'd met Mr. or Ms. Right in much less than a year while 30 percent say let it play through the four seasons. A third of both men and women figure between twelve and twenty-four months is the right amount of time to really know someone, and 11 percent believe in being really sure—in two to three years. Six percent say you need even longer.

EVER FOUND IT TOUGH DATING SOMEONE FROM A DIFFERENT ECONOMIC LEVEL?

Two-thirds of daters insist they've never felt uncomfortable or uneasy dating someone much richer or poorer. There's been more hesitation about dating someone from a different class, however.

EVER DATED SOMEONE FROM A DIFFERENT CLASS?

Assuming level of education is the class divider, crossing over is not too common. In 2000, 94 percent of married high school dropouts were married to someone else who had either also dropped out or had only a high school diploma. More than two out of three married adults with advanced degrees had spouses with at least a bachelor's degree. Less than 1 percent of those with advanced degrees had a spouse who did not complete high school.

HOW ABOUT FROM A DIFFERENT RACE?

Maybe it's PC posturing or maybe young folks really have embraced the "we are one world" concept. Seventy-eight percent of us say, sure, why not, if James Bond can get it on with Halle Berry, why can't we? Another 15 percent aren't so sure, while 6 percent cannot foresee it in their future. Thirteen percent of people avow they've dated someone of another race many times, while 29 percent admit to doing so once. But 56 percent have never done so. Few of the dates lead anywhere. Interracial marriages make up just 3 percent of all unions.

HOW ABOUT A DIFFERENT RELIGION?

Few people object to casual dating of someone of a different religion. Only 42 percent of single young adults feel it is important to find a spouse who shares their religion.

WOULD YOU DATE A WOMAN FIVE YEARS OLDER THAN YOU?

Eighty-nine percent of men would willingly date a woman up to five years his senior.

WOULD YOU DATE SOMEONE YOU FIND PHYSICALLY UNATTRACTIVE?

Three out of five women (59 percent) would go out with someone who doesn't turn them on—though the degree of turnoff is critical—but only 46 percent of men would go out with someone they don't consider seductive. Four out of five women admit they can be courted by a less than perfect specimen.

WOULD YOU DATE SOMEONE WHOSE YOUNG KIDS LIVED WITH THEM?

This one's a coin toss. An equal number of men (47 percent) say yes as those who say they wouldn't willingly get into this arrangement. And interestingly, an equal number of women (40 percent) are open to it as who call it a door-closer. At the same time, 74 percent of women say they're open to dating a dad and 60 percent of men said what's most important in dating a mom is that she knows that her children come first.

WOULD YOU DATE A SMOKER?

Half of women claim they have no reluctance dating someone who smokes cigarettes (cigars are another matter) but 90 percent of men would rather not travel tobacco road.

✗WOULD YOU DATE SOMEONE WITH A SEXUALLY TRANSMITTED DISEASE?

For 38 percent of people an STD would be a deal-breaker but 36 percent think they would be able to see beyond that. One in four can't imagine how they would react given the situation.

WOULD YOU HOOK UP WITH SOMEONE WHO HAD A LOW SEX DRIVE?

Men are virtually equally split on this front, with the same percent saying yes as saying no. Women are considerably more forgiving with virtually twice as many seeing a low sex drive as no obstacle to a happy relationship.

WOULD YOU ENTER INTO A RELATIONSHIP WITH A FRIEND'S ESTRANGED SPOUSE?

Few even questioned whether the friendship was a close one: 84 percent consider such an arrangement strictly taboo.

✗ HOW IMPORTANT IS IT THAT THE GUY BE TALLER THAN THE WOMAN IN A RELATIONSHIP?

A third of men say they'd be more comfortable with a woman who is shorter—as would a third of women. The rest consider height differentials irrelevant.

✗ WOULD YOU RATHER DATE SOMEONE BROKE BUT BIG-HEARTED, OR RICH BUT UGLY?

The poor man with the rich heart trumps the rich man with the poor looks by more than a three-to-one margin.

✗ HOW IMPORTANT ARE YOUR PARTNER'S FINANCES?

For 64 percent of women, a man's income—and more important his income potential—is critical, but only 23 percent of men put much value on a woman's finances.

✗ HAVE YOU EVER BROKEN UP WITH SOMEONE BECAUSE OF FAMILY PRESSURE?

Fifteen percent of us have ended a relationship because parents have objected to the partner. Thirty-seven percent admit (perhaps somewhat ruefully) that they have at least once in life broken someone's heart.

✗ HOW DO YOU DRESS ON A FIRST DATE?

For four out of five first-timers the optimal word is comfort—they wear whatever makes them feel relaxed and confident in a potentially unsettling situation. Ten percent buy something special for the occasion. Three out of four women dab some scent on as do 58 percent of men. Some 15 percent of men admit they actively fret about how they smell.

✗ SO WHAT ELSE ARE YOU WORRIED ABOUT ON A DATE?

Four out of five guys worry most about their date having a good time. Second biggest worry (56 percent) is if she thinks they are acting like a geek. Just 18 percent of men worry about ending up a father after a big date.

✗ DO YOU USUALLY DO ANYTHING OUT OF THE ORDINARY TO GET READY FOR A DATE?

Women are significantly likelier than men to put on special undergarments (33 percent vs. 13 percent), and clean their house or apartment (58 percent vs. 52 percent). Two out of three guys and 54 percent of women stop at the bank or ATM for extra cash, 42 percent of men wash their car, and 25 percent buy flowers or candy.

DO YOU HAVE AN ESCAPE PLAN IN MIND IF IT'S NOT UP TO SNUFF?

If you're left waiting at the table for twenty minutes, figure you've been dumped. Twenty-two percent of women hatch a plan to get out of a bad date, twice the percentage of men who've got an out up their sleeve.

WHO SHOULD CALL WHOM AFTER A GOOD FIRST DATE?

The etiquette jury is still out: 71 percent of women say they've no qualms about making the first call. But even those who decide to play coy won't have long to wait. The majority of guys (64 percent) say they'll call within a day, 29 percent will call two to three days afterward, and 2 percent will wait four days before calling.

ARE YOU GENERALLY A NERVOUS NELLY ON A FIRST DATE?

Almost all of us (93 percent) experience jitters on a first date and 66 percent admit they've had many interludes of awkward silences. Fifty-one percent say they've felt trapped and unable to leave when they didn't like someone. One in four women claim to be disillusioned with dating.

FURNITURE-SHOP TOGETHER OR MEET THE PARENTS?

Thirty-eight percent of bachelors consider furniture-shopping with their honeys a bigger sign of commitment than meeting her parents.

HAVE YOU EVER ISSUED AN ULTIMATUM?

Eleven percent of women and 3 percent of men confess they've forced their partner to make a choice: marry or move out. Statistical evidence suggests that these do-or-die scenarios more often backfire than succeed.

WHAT'S THE WORST DAY TO BE DATELESS?

Saturday nights come and go but New Year's Eve occurs once every 365 days. Twenty-eight percent of singles are more pained spending that night alone than any other.

EVER GONE FROM FRIEND TO LOVER?

Forty-seven percent of couples were friends for more than a year before notching up the relationship.

IS CHIVALRY DEAD?

Most single men in North America like observing the old-fashioned gestures: 91 percent try to open doors for dates, 85 percent prefer to pick up the tab, and 77 percent would like to help their date put on her coat. But 29 percent of both men and women say that whoever is nearest the swinging door should hold it, and closest to the elevator door should exit. Manners haven't gone out of business; they've just become gender neutral. Four percent see men who go out of their way to hold the door as pandering.

WHAT DO YOU EXPECT FROM YOUR MAN ON THE MANNERS FRONT?

Twenty-three percent of women expect their dates to open car doors for them and hang up their coats. Only 22 percent of women anticipate their dates will pull out their chairs for them. And 5 percent of women say they wouldn't be peeved if their dates flirted with the waitress.

IS IT OKAY FOR A WOMAN TO ASK A MAN FOR HIS TELEPHONE NUMBER? A DATE?

Four out of five women say yes on both counts, but just 55 percent of women feel comfortable asking a guy for a date. Sixty-two percent of women say they have at least once initiated the offer. Thirty-five percent of the time he was flattered but 19 percent of the time, the asker felt humiliated.

EVER FELT PRESSURED TO DO MORE THAN YOU WANT BY A DATE?

Some 58 percent say no—that they don't and wouldn't date people who would do that. Twenty-nine percent sense something like this happened but they handled it successfully. Meanwhile, 8 percent acknowledge giving in to the pressure and doing something that they later regretted. Three percent admit they were the ones doing the pressuring.

HAVE YOU EVER BEEN PHYSICALLY OR SEXUALLY ABUSED BY A DATE?

The vast majority of us (92 percent) say no. But 3 percent admit to having been physically hurt and 2 percent sexually hurt. One percent were hurt both physically and sexually.

HOW LONG DO MOST "BETWEEN RELATIONSHIPS" LAST?

The average "hang time" between romances is 11.5 months for women, considerable, but shy of the fifteen months average between serious relationships for men. The average wait for sex is just over four months.

HAVE YOU EVER AGREED TO A DATE BECAUSE YOU LIKED THE CAR HE WAS DRIVING?

Shallow as it is, 7.5 percent of women say they're guilty as charged.

WHEN A POPULAR GIRL SAYS ON THURSDAY THAT SHE'S BUSY SATURDAY, DO YOU BELIEVE IT?

That's not the message 47 percent of guys hear; they think she's playing hard to get. And 28 percent dismiss her as a *Rules* girl and not someone they'd call back. Just one in four take that rejection as a sign that she's highly sought after.

DOES GOING OUT OF TOWN TOGETHER FOR THE WEEKEND MEAN SOMETHING?

It's a big deal for 63 percent of daters; they consider it an indication of serious intent. Thirty-one percent see it as a significant stepping-stone because they're investing time. But 6 percent regard it just like any other date.

WOULD YOU GO TO A STRIP CLUB WITH YOUR GUY?

If their beaus wanted to go, 86 percent of women would join them. Fourteen percent would not, considering that a decidedly uncool place for couples. Seventeen percent of men agree.

EVER LIE TO GET A DATE?

Amazingly, one in two guys admits he would and has. The top three things they fib about include their willingness to commit, their interest in more than just sex, and their income. *Men's Health* found the average guy is 57 percent more likely to lie if the woman is pretty. Equally amazing is that one in three women also misrepresent, primarily about their looks.

SATISFIED WITH THE AMOUNT OF DATING YOU'RE DOING . . . AND THE DATES THEMSELVES?

Despite the population disparity, it's women who tend to be more satisfied with the amount of dating they're doing compared to men (43 percent vs. 32 percent). Women looking for love are also more satisfied with the quality of their dating compared to men (41 percent vs. 35 percent). But overall, 47 percent of men and 46 percent of women consider many of the dates they go on to be miserable experiences.

FIND THAT RETURNING TO THE DATING SCENE WAS A BIT LIKE RIDING A BICYCLE?

Although we never forget how to do it only a small percent of us transition back without complication. Most reenter this land with unresolved hurts: self-esteem issues and traumas from past relationships. Some don't feel dating again is worth the effort and are prepared to go at life alone. It's not the norm for first-timers but those out on the dating scene again after a long perch often feel it's hopeless.

EXPECT YOU'LL FIND THE RELATIONSHIP YOU'RE LOOKING FOR?

That depends on how old you are. Younger people are more optimistic about finding the perfect match but grow increasingly disillusioned as they age. Sixty-one percent of seventeen- to twenty-five-year-olds expect to find what they're looking for, compared to just 16 percent of those over fifty-five. Roughly half the population believe they'll connect with a love but 54 percent of men and 61 percent of women suspect they'll remain single forever, failing to meet Mr. or Ms. Right.

5

Speaking of Sex

GETTING ENOUGH?

Almost a third of men and a quarter of women have unsated appetites. For most of us, thirteen times a month sounds like the right amount. Three out of four men (71.4 percent) claim they get turned on daily, compared with 34 percent of women. The rest of the men feel the urge twice a week or so, along with 44.7 percent of women.

HOW MUCH IS ENOUGH?

Every day, people worldwide make love about 120 million times, resulting in 910,000 pregnancies. Per head, that breaks down to an average of 106 times a year. It's not just guns, jets, and butter that Americans have the most of: they also have more sex—on average 132 times a year, with Russians close behind at 122 times a year, the French at 121, and the Greeks at 115. According to Durex, it's the Japanese who have sex least often, at 37 times a year on average, followed by the Malaysians (62) and Chinese (69). Liberals are twice as likely as conservatives to make love more than once a day. Couples living together overall have more sex than marrieds—146 vs. 98

times a year. Singles have the least—on average 49 times a year. Four percent of people claim to do it daily and 57 percent at least once a week.

WHY THE SHORTFALL?

Headaches are no longer the most offered excuse: nowadays, it's plain fatigue and logistics standing in the way.

DID JUNIOR'S ARRIVAL HAVE ANYTHING TO DO WITH IT?

It did for 72 percent of new parents—28 percent because they lost their privacy and 44 percent because they lost their energy. But 28 percent saw no cooling down of their sex life after the kids were born. Even though doctors advise it, roughly half of couples don't abstain for the whole six weeks after birth. Hey, that's part of the celebration.

HOW LONG HAS THIS BEEN GOING ON?

Counting foreplay—and apparently the whole seduction process as well as the actual act—people clock their average sexual experience at thirty-nine minutes. With a long-standing partner, the average encounter usually runs less, say sixteen minutes, and a fourth of us say their most frequent sessions take no more than ten minutes.

DO YOU THINK SEX IMPROVES WITH AGE?

The quantity probably won't, but the quality most likely will. A National Council on Aging survey reports that of those still doing it at age sixty, at least 70 percent consider their sex lives more satisfying than when they were forty.

HOW DO YOU FEEL ABOUT GETTING AND GIVING ORAL SEX?

About half of us still wince about giving oral sex and about a third demur receiving it. While 19 percent of women say they're regularly on the receiving end of oral sex, 46 percent say they would like to be! Four out of five say they truly enjoy going down there; 72 percent contend they're turned on by the smell and taste of a woman.

HOW PSYCHOLOGICALLY IN CONTROL DO YOU FEEL GIVING ORAL SEX?

Ah, here's the silver lining: 36 percent of women absolutely relish the power it gives them while another third recognize it puts them in the driver's seat.

DO YOU SWALLOW THE SEMEN WHEN YOU GIVE ORAL SEX?

Half never do, and another fourth don't swallow every time. Fewer than one in five say they actually enjoy doing so. Thirty-seven percent of guys wish their partners would swallow, interpreting it as a sign of devotion. Slightly more are so grateful that they don't care, and one in four wonder why on earth she would—they certainly wouldn't.

DOES THE SIZE OF HIS MEMBER AFFECT YOUR SEXUAL SATISFACTION?

Three-fifths of women (61 percent) say size matters, with 43 percent claiming that longer *and* wider are better. One in five (22 percent) said width is really all that matters, and 6 percent claim length is the key.

ARE YOU PUT OFF FROM SEX WHEN YOU HAVE YOUR PERIOD?

Not likely. The drive is stronger than the mess. Two out of three men say they're perfectly happy having sex during a women's menstruation while 10 percent of women refrain for either religious or laundry reasons.

DO YOU ASK FOR WHAT YOU WANT?

Amazingly, men and women alike may know what they want in the pleasure zone, but they can't or won't ask for it. While three out of four women crave more foreplay, only 57 percent feel they could make that request. And while two out of three men long for oral sex, only half could tell their partners how much they'd like some more lip.

GUYS, DO YOU ENJOY IT WHEN SHE TELLS YOU WHAT TO DO IN BED?

More than four out of five (83 percent) say they love it when their partner plays drill sergeant in the sack.

WOULD YOU WELCOME YOUR PARTNER ASKING "HOW'S THIS?" EVERY STEP OF THE WAY?

Four out of every five men and 68 percent of women say they'd really enjoy it if their partner solicited a does-that-feel-good blow-by-blow reaction during sex.

HOW KINKY ARE YOU?

Someone is buying all those whips and chains. Five percent of us claim we're into bondage. Almost one in five of us (18 percent) regularly use pornographic material to spice up the sex act and more than one in ten (11 percent) use some sort of sexual toy—vibrators, electric toothbrushes, you name it. Twenty-two percent of men and 18 percent of women regard fetish behavior as normal.

WHAT'S THE SEXIEST FEATURE ON A PARTNER OR PROSPECT?

They say the eyes are the window to the soul and gateway to our hearts. Sixty-nine percent consider them a person's sexiest feature, while 19 percent are captured by his or her mouth. Twelve percent think the hands are a person's sexiest attribute.

WHAT'S THE BEST GIFT TO SAY "I LOVE YOU"?

More of us consider flowers and houseplants to be the best gift to express love (37 percent), followed by jewelry (34 percent) and scent (5 percent).

WHAT IS MOST ESSENTIAL FOR GREAT SEX?

A willingness to try anything and good oral sex technique are tied at the top (22 percent), followed by a sense of humor in bed (16 percent), and a large penis (13 percent). For 13 percent, a good body is critical, while for 10 percent it's stamina.

WHICH WOULD YOU MOST LIKELY DO FIRST: ORAL SEX OR INTERCOURSE?

Most of us would engage in oral sex first, but not by a landslide: 37.7 percent for women and 48.5 percent for men. A third of women (33.3 percent) and 17.6 percent of men expect intercourse would happen first and 29 percent of women and 34 percent of men say they'd kick in oral sex around the same time.

WHAT'S YOUR FAVORITE TIME FOR SEX?

For 19 percent it's the morning, 4 percent midday, 6 percent the afternoon, and 30 percent like the evening best of all. But 38 percent say time hardly matters, that all are satisfying. Saturday night is the favorite evening for North Americans to have sex and more orgasms occur at 10:34 P.M. than at any other time of the week.

DO YOU TALK TO YOUR FRIENDS ABOUT YOUR SEX LIFE?

Only 12.6 percent of women are mum on the subject vs. 27.2 percent of men. Another 28.7 percent of men only discuss it in a very vague, general way. Twenty-six percent of men and 30 percent of women confess they find it difficult to talk about sex at all.

DO YOU READ SELF-HELP SEX BOOKS?

Forty-four percent of people admit they have done so.

HOW DO YOU LET YOUR PARTNER KNOW YOU'RE HORNY?

Fifty-four percent of women and 62 percent of men say they put the moves on their partner, while 14 percent of women and 20 percent of men ask for it verbally. Nineteen percent of women say they act really sexy and irresistible and 12 percent of both sexes suffer in silence waiting for their partner to figure it out.

HOW DO YOU FEEL WHEN YOUR PARTNER DOESN'T CLIMAX BUT YOU DO?

Forty-two percent are okay with one coming and the other not, as long as their partners are fine with it. Fifteen percent are content with it under any circumstances. The rest are disappointed: 25 percent wishing they were more skillful and 18 percent wishing their partners were more responsive.

LADIES, WHAT'S THE MOST SEXUALLY RESPONSIVE PART OF YOUR BODY?

For 38 percent of women breasts and nipples beat out the clitoris (28 percent). As for the most sensitive place to be kissed, that's a toss-up between the ear and inner thigh, each corralling 40 percent of the vote. Only 20 percent point to the lips.

GUYS, WHAT SEX TECHNIQUE CAUSES YOU GREAT STRESS?

Timing the climax is the big one, according to 47 percent of guys. Another 21 percent are stressed out by not knowing the proper thing to do after. Fourteen percent are antsy about giving oral sex and 6 percent about receiving it. Four percent are on shaky ground about whether they're doing the initial penetration smoothly and 4 percent wonder about their kissing etiquette.

DO YOU LIKE IT WHEN A GIRL TAKES CONTROL IN BED?

For 2 percent of control freaks it's a downer. But 57 percent find a dominant woman a real turn-on and 42 percent appreciate it, as long as they know each other well.

GUYS, HOW SKILLFUL ARE YOU AT REMOVING A WOMAN'S BRA?

Forty percent of men are all thumbs, spending an average of twenty-seven seconds taking a bra off using both hands. In a timed test, right-handed men using their left hand took an average of fifty-eight seconds. Lacy, plain, cotton, or silk, at some point bras have turned lustful young lads into blithering bumbledorfs.

GUYS, DID YOU HAVE WET DREAMS?

You don't have them now, of course, but adolescent boys have as many as a dozen wet dreams a week. The average age of first ejaculation among boys is thirteen years and two months.

DID YOU LEARN FROM A MAESTRO?

One in five men have been indoctrinated into the joys of sex at the hands of a woman at least ten years their senior. Thirteen percent lost their virginity this way. Only 9 percent of women have been in such a relationship.

WHAT'S LOVE GOT TO DO WITH IT?

Forty-six percent of guys and gals claim they don't have to love a person to sleep with him or her but 31 percent are of the exact opposite mind. Twenty-three percent would not sleep with someone whom they had no plan to see again.

6

Pucker Up

Anthropologists believe kissing began in the Stone Age when human cave-dwelling mothers transferred food from their mouths to their babies' mouths, and adults mimicked it. Nowadays there are innumerable variants, such as the blown kiss that flies across a crowded room, the platonic peck on the cheek, the Hollywood air kiss, the lip-lock, the French kiss, and the vacuum kiss. So pucker up!

IS A KISS JUST A KISS?
A sigh may be just a sigh but a kiss can speak volumes. Three out of four women and half of men think kissing is more intimate than sex itself. If love makes the world go around, two pairs of lips meeting is an essential part of the process, according to 77 percent of people. It could mean nothing—or everything—depending on the circumstances. Fewer than one in five of us consider it anything more than a twenty-six-calorie-burner that raises our blood pressure and nourishes our body with extra oxygen. Twenty-four percent consider someone's kissing ability an indication of sexual prowess. And 85 percent of Americans consider it the most sensual activity around.

HOW SKILLFUL A KISSER ARE YOU?
Fully 49 percent rate their own kissing prowess as eight or better on a scale of one to ten.

DO YOU PRACTICE KISSING?
Anthropologist Helen E. Fisher says nine out of ten people world-wide practice kissing in some form—like into their pillows.

WHEN DID YOU HAVE YOUR FIRST REAL KISS?
Men start earlier with an equal percent recalling it at between thirteen to fifteen as between sixteen to eighteen. Nine percent were late to pucker; waiting until they were nineteen or older to experience a real romantic smooch. At the same time, 42 percent of women had their first real kiss at sixteen, while 15 percent were at least twenty-one.

DO YOU LIKE FRENCH KISSING? VACUUM KISSING?
Mais oui, say 99 percent of us, but not all the time. Most women don't think it's appropriate in the early stage of a relationship. As for the vacuum kiss, 75 percent of people have never sucked the air out of their partner's mouth and lungs.

WHAT'S THE BEST KIND OF KISS?
It's a toss-up between a sexy, long, fun kiss and a sweet, soft, romantic one. Ten percent also say the best kind is the first kiss.

WHAT'S MOST LIKELY TO RUIN A KISSING MOMENT?
Bad breath, say 43 percent, while 29 percent say the magic of the moment can vanish when it's interrupted. Sixteen percent think an overaggressive partner can gum up the works and 7 percent say hands going where they shouldn't can ruin the moment. For 41 percent of people the worst part about a bad kiss is tongue-tangling followed by lips that are too wet and biting.

WHAT MAKES A PERSON A BAD KISSER?
Sloppy saliva and lips that are too wet, contend 38 percent of us. While 22 percent say an overabundance of tongue is the problem, 8 percent say not enough tongue ruins it for them. Twelve percent claim teeth getting in the way and biting are hallmarks of bad kissing.

WHAT MAKES A PERSON A GOOD KISSER?

More than a third (34 percent) say soft lips and 30 percent indicate light tongue movement. Twenty-one percent consider gentle pressure the key and 9 percent, firm pressure. Eight-four percent of women and 78 percent of men claim they like being gently bitten on the lips while kissing.

IS LIPSTICK LOVABLE?

After diamonds it may be a woman's best friend, but 37 percent of men prefer lips with nothing on them but their own. Of those who like lipstick, 19 percent prefer really red shades, with pale pink coming in third. As for flavors, strawberry is the most popular (23 percent), followed by champagne (21 percent), and peppermint (18 percent).

DO YOU LIKE HAVING YOUR FEET KISSED? HOW ABOUT NECK AND EARS?

Only 3 percent of people confess they're into having their feet focused on. Ninety-seven percent of women and 10 percent of men enjoy having their necks kissed, while 94 percent of women and 55 percent of men enjoy the buss on their ears. Men aren't turned on by belly kisses (go lower, they beg) but 3 percent of women love to be kissed on their tummies.

DO YOU PREFER TO KISS WITH YOUR EYES OPEN OR SHUT?

Roughly a third of men and women (38 and 30 percent respectively) prefer to look at whom they're kissing.

DO YOU SLANT TO THE RIGHT OR LEFT WHEN KISSING?

Almost two out of three (64.5 percent) people slant their heads to the right when kissing—roughly the same proportion who are right-handed.

DO YOU LIKE KISSING OUT IN THE OPEN?

Provided the kiss isn't too intimate, lengthy or deep, 94 percent of people like to be kissed in public.

EVER CRY FROM KISSING?

When it feels excruciatingly good 2 percent of people even cry.

LADIES, DO YOU ENJOY KISSING MEN WITH MUSTACHES AND BEARDS?

Tickling is part of the fun, 40 percent of women say. But given the choice, four our of five women would rather that their partners be clean shaven.

WHERE IS THE MOST ROMANTIC PLACE TO KISS?

The canopy of stars wins hands down: 58 percent like kissing outside at night. But 19 percent of people also consider the beach anytime of day a romantic venue and 11 percent opt for the top of the Ferris wheel. Four percent say parked in the car is quite romantic. Movies are also popular: a 1997 Princeton University study concluded that our brains are equipped with neurons that help us find our lovers' lips in the dark.

WHO SHOULD START THE KISSING BALL ROLLING?

The guy, according to four out of five of us. But when he's too shy to start, the women should step up to the plate. Once the first kiss has occurred, then it's fair game for anyone to initiate a second . . . and so on.

IS MOST OF YOUR KISSING A PRELUDE TO SEX?

Fewer than one in five people concede they use kissing as a way to start the ball rolling. For the rest it's a form of affection to be done anywhere.

DO YOU BELIEVE THAT KISSING SOMEONE UNDER THE MISTLETOE BRINGS GOOD LUCK?

One in four of us hold that truth to be self-evident.

DO YOU USUALLY KISS GOOD-BYE WHEN SETTING OFF FOR THE DAY?

Two out of three of us usually peck the cheek or brush the lips of our partners before setting off for work. Yet 17 percent of women and 4 percent of men in relationships claim they never kiss their mates good-bye for such routine partings.

DO YOU USUALLY KISS GOOD NIGHT?

It's as omnipresent as the smiley face used to be, and about as meaningful. Nine out of ten people in happy relationships kiss those
around them good night, but it's almost universally a clichéd symbol
rather than meaningful moment.

HOW MUCH TIME DO YOU THINK YOU SPEND KISSING?

It's been estimated that the average person spends two weeks of his
or her lifetime kissing—or 4.36 hours a year. Broken down that's a
mere five minutes a week, assuming a life expectancy of seventy-
seven.

IF A PROSPECT ISN'T A GOOD KISSER, DOES THAT RULE HIM OR HER OUT?

Fifty-three percent of us would give the bad kisser another chance—
assuming they could teach that old dog new tricks.

WHAT'S THE MOST MEMORABLE KISS IN MOVIE HISTORY?

Rhett Butler and Scarlet O'Hara did it best in *Gone with the Wind*,
followed by the beach kiss between Burt Lancaster and Deborah Kerr
in *From Here to Eternity*.

DO YOU THINK KISSING IMPROVES WITH MARRIAGE?

Many think so because of the heightened intimacy but 51 percent
say that kissing becomes routine after the knot is tied. On the other
hand, it may have real benefits. German psychologists believe that
couples who kiss each morning miss less work because of illness than
those who do not, have fewer car accidents on the way to work, earn
more, and live longer. The point is that a morning kiss begins the
day with a positive attitude.

7

When It Comes to Sex,
Do You Usually . . .

GET THE BALL ROLLING?
Maybe it's to salve their egos but 43 percent of men and 45 percent of women say they both initiate equally. When one does so more than the other, it's guys almost twice as often as women who get things going.

DO IT AT NIGHT?
The most popular time for sex is late Saturday evening. The least aphrodisiacal time—or at least the time when folks are least likely to be going at it—is early Monday afternoon.

DIM THE LIGHTS OR LIGHT CANDLES?
The average guy has sex with the lights off, although he'd rather have them on. But that's a concession to women who overwhelmingly prefer to do it in the dark.

TRY OUT NEW POSITIONS?

Only one in four people admit to being in a rut. The rest say they regularly turn up the heat by trying new sexual positions.

PLAY MUSIC?

If there's time, and the scene is being set, so to speak, most of us plop in a CD. Jazz is the preferred accompaniment (26 percent), followed by rhythm and blues (24), rock 'n' roll (18 percent), blues (16 percent), and classical (11 percent). Four percent opt for white noise.

BRUSH YOUR TEETH BEFORE?

Even 28 percent of those bright-eyed and bushy-tailed lovers who get busy before the skies brighten brush their teeth.

REACH ORGASM?

Just 15 percent of women and 2 percent of men sadly say they usually don't. Men say they've achieved orgasm in nine of the last ten sex acts; women bat seven out of ten.

HAVE AN ORGASM MORE THAN ONCE EACH SESSION?

Some 38 percent of women and 16 percent of men claim they usually have multiple orgasms.

CLIMAX AT THE SAME TIME AS YOUR PARTNER?

A University of Wisconsin study found that 17 percent of partners come at approximately the same moment as each other, while 40 percent of the time, women precede their mate. Another 31 percent wait, either voluntarily or otherwise, for their turn. One in four men (24 percent) think they need to climax simultaneously for great sex but just around half of women feel that way.

HOW LONG DOES YOUR ORGASM LAST?

It may seem like an eternity but the typical male orgasm lasts anywhere from three to eight seconds. Deep breathing and regular exercising can extend that to perhaps ten seconds. Women can keep on climaxing without rest in between; their sustained orgasm can last twenty to sixty seconds. But it takes the average woman twenty-seven minutes to reach orgasm compared to eleven minutes for a man.

TALK DURING SEX?
Twenty-six percent of women and 29 percent of men claim they rarely chat while going at it. Just 12 percent of both men and women say it's part of their routine.

HONOR RITUALS?
Most of us do. For example, more than a third of male football fans abstain from sex the night before a big match.

USE LINGERIE SHREWDLY?
Half of us (49 percent) claim to wear lingerie to spice things up. But 68 percent of women say their prime purpose in wearing lingerie is to please themselves.

TELL YOUR PARTNER WHAT YOU LIKE?
Eighty-four percent claim they aren't shy about telling their partners about their sexual preferences, although 61 percent do so only rarely or occasionally.

THINK ABOUT SOMETHING ELSE?
Live in the moment. More of us (35 percent of men and 36 percent of women) go politically correct here, claiming to think only of their partners. But 9 percent of men and 5 percent of women say they're often musing about somebody else. Three percent of men admit their mind wanders to other pleasures (like baseball) and pains (like tax returns), while 7 percent of women confess that thoughts of shopping or getting the washing machine fixed cross their minds.

SQUIRT DURING ORGASM, GALS?
Two out of five women ejaculate at least sometimes during orgasm. While semen can spray one to two feet—remember the hilarious scene in *There's Something about Mary*?—female juices are more like seepage.

GO IN AND OUT A LOT?
The average session involves ninety in-and-out thrusts—alas burning a mere two calories per minute.

DO IT MISSIONARY STYLE?

Arabs call it "the manner of serpents." In Tuscany, it's known as the "angelic position." For three out of four of us, the woman lying down on her back with the male on top is the default position. One in five lovers almost always do it that way, while fewer than 10 percent rarely or never do. The rest do so with varying frequency but for most it is a mainstay. Even so, 6.6 percent of people say they have difficulty achieving orgasm this way.

GO WITH THE WOMAN ON TOP?

All together 54 percent have this position in their occasionally used repertoire but 11.6 percent do it that way all the time and 9.1 percent rarely or never do. Interestingly, for 23 percent of women this position is an orgasm guarantee.

DO IT "DOGGY STYLE?"

For 28 percent of women doggy style is a surefire way to reach orgasm and 40 percent say it allows for deep penetration. Just 14.4 percent of lovers rarely if ever do this while 9.1 percent gravitate to this virtually every time they have sex.

ANSWER THE PHONE WHEN YOU'RE "BUSY?"

Almost half of men and women say never, but an equal number claim it depends on how advanced the action is. Twelve percent of women and 7 percent of men say they routinely respond to the telephone.

CUDDLE AFTER?

Cuddling is the big thing for both men and women (34 and 42 percent respectively), followed by sleep (25 and 14 percent). Thirteen percent of women and 10.6 percent of men light up a cigarette and 12.3 percent of women wash up. Eleven percent of men and women talk and 4.5 percent eat or drink.

WATCH TV?

According to the FBI (why would they be studying this, you wonder?) 19 percent of all couples turn on the television after sex, and a third have it on during the action.

GET READY TO DO IT AGAIN RIGHT AWAY?

That's another thing that depends on age. Eighteen-year-old stud muffins are ready for action again in fifteen minutes; septuagenarians need around twenty hours to recharge. The average guy is refreshed in a half hour.

SCREAM OUT YOUR PARTNER'S NAME IN BED?

Expand the answer to "moan" and the percentage jumps. Twentynine percent of women and 25 percent of men say they often whisper, whimper, sigh, or cry out the name of their partner when seized by passion.

PREFER A STRIPTEASE TO UNDRESSING YOUR PARTNER?

Most people like to mix it up but a third of both men and women say they like it better when their partner makes a show of undressing.

TICKLE YOUR PARTNER UNTIL HE OR SHE BEGS YOU TO STOP?

What fun, proclaim 44 percent of women and 49 percent of men.

USE A PET NAME FOR YOUR GENITALS?

Thirty-six percent of men and 30 percent of women have cutesy names for their organs. Big Jim and the twins; Excalibur, Otis, Quasimodo, Scud Missile, the Big Easy, Weasel, Thor, and Wilbur are some of the more common monikers.

CLIMAX DURING ORAL SEX?

Just 42 percent of women say they do.

TALK DIRTY?

Amazingly, it's women letting loose more than men (74 percent vs. 58 percent). Sixty-one percent of us like this heat-inspired language but 16 percent find it funny or revolting. Another 22 percent feel too inhibited to try such self-expression.

SCHEDULE SESSIONS?

For those in regular relationships just 6.6 percent of women and 8.5 percent of men say they more often schedule sex than let it happen spontaneously, although 25 percent of women and 27 percent of men admit there's a bit of both in their relationships.

USE IT TO GET WHAT YOU WANT?
They've been doing it since Aristophanes wrote *Lysistrata*. A fourth of women (25 percent) admit they withhold sex—or confer it—to influence their partners but 85 percent of guys profess to never having done so. (Maybe because sex is what they want?)

DOUCHE RIGHT AFTER?
About a third of women twenty to thirty years old still do, even though doctors discourage it.

INCORPORATE EXOTIC CLOTHES IN YOUR LOVEMAKING?
Ninety-two percent of heterosexual women say they do, or would like to.

USE VAGINAL LUBRICANTS?
Two out of five (40 percent) couples do.

GET SPRING FEVER?
For 86 percent of us, when winter wanes and warm weather is in the air, romance is on our minds. Just 14 percent claim to be impervious to the weather's effects on their romantic sensibilities.

ENJOY EROTIC MASSAGE?
Seventy-seven percent of women and 84 percent of men say pounding the flesh is a great way to get the sparks flying.

TELL YOUR PARTNER THAT HE OR SHE IS SEXY?
Sixty-four percent of us do.

WAKE IN THE MORNING WITH A HARD-ON, GUYS?
Pretty often it seems. A third do so one to three times a week and almost 20 percent three to five times. More than 15 percent claim to do so every day.

8

When It Comes to Sex,
Have You Ever . . .

DONE IT WITH SOMEONE BECAUSE YOU FELT SORRY FOR HIM OR HER?
Twenty-seven percent of men and a third of women admit they have been good sexual Samaritans.

PARTICIPATED IN CASUAL SEX BETWEEN FRIENDS?
It's a big tension reliever—and maybe a portal to more, say most of the four out of ten folks who've done it. Some, however, have found it damaged the friendship.

DONE IT WITH A COMPLETE STRANGER?
Some 39 percent of men and a quarter of women admitted they had. And 26 percent of women and 32 percent of men confess they've slept with someone whose name they didn't know, some, more than once. Thirty-five percent of men claim it's not their style, as do 58 percent of women.

PAID FOR IT?
One in three American men have had sex with a prostitute at least once in their lives. And 7 percent of men over fifty admit they've had at least one such contact since the age of fifty.

SLEPT WITH SOMEONE DUE TO DRUNKENESS?
Half of women and 52 percent of men admit that they have, some, more than once.

HAD ORAL SEX DONE ON YOU, GALS?
Amazingly, 95 percent of women report that they have, and 94 percent enjoyed it.

DONE IT ON THE FLOOR?
More than half of women (58.6 percent) and almost as many men (47.5 percent) have even experienced rug burn on their back or butt from it. Just 11 percent of folks say they've never done it on the floor.

HAD MORE THAN ONE SEXUAL PARTNER ON THE SAME DAY?
It's happened for 42 percent of men and 44 percent of women. While 41 percent of women say they would never do that, only 23 percent of men share that view.

HAD TWO SEXUAL RELATIONSHIPS GOING SIMULTANEOUSLY?
Almost a third of men (31 percent) say they have but just 14 percent of women own up to that.

STARTED CRYING IN THE MIDDLE OF THE ACT?
Thirty-five percent of men and 23 percent of women say that they or their partners have become tearful during lovemaking.

STARTED GIGGLING?
Could be either from passing a little gas or the slapping of bellies with the sweat between them, but half of men and 81 percent of women say they have started laughing uncontrollably during the act.

EXPERIENCED GOD IN A MOMENT OF SEXUAL ECSTASY?

Fifty-eight percent of those sixty and older say they have, compared with only 23 percent of those thirty and under.

INITIATED IT WHILE YOUR PARTNER WAS ASLEEP?

No one is accusing them of necrophilia but two thirds of men and 55 percent of women say they have made advances on a sleeping partner.

FALLEN ASLEEP DURING THE ACT?

Who doesn't like a good nap? Twenty-eight percent of women and a third of men admit they've dozed off during the doings.

HAD VIRTUAL SEX?

A third of us have.

TAKEN THE MORNING-AFTER PILL?

One percent of women have.

SAID NO WHEN YOU REALLY WANTED IT AND GAVE THE SIGNALS YOU DID?

Thirty-seven percent of women admit they've uttered token resistance—said no even when they wanted sex.

TASTED YOURSELF?

Who needs the golden arches? Three out of four women (74 percent) and 65 percent of men say their curiosity got the best of them—that they have at least once tasted their own vaginal secretions or semen. Eleven percent of women and 18 percent of men find the thought revolting.

CALLED A SEX PHONE LINE?

Only 16 percent of females and 19 percent of males admit they have been this horny.

DONE IT IN A BED WITH PLASTIC SHEETS?

Only 10 percent of women and 9 percent of men have prepared for sex's effusions in this way.

DONE IT IN FRONT OF SOMEONE WHO PAID TO WATCH?

Very few of us have actually done that, but almost half of men say they would accept the offer to be paid for doing what comes naturally and 42 percent of women would go along with that.

BOUGHT OR RENTED A PORN MOVIE?

Despite the loudness of the Moral Majority's cry, more than one in five of us (22 percent) have rented a porn flick at least once. And 5.4 billion of them sold in one recent year.

TRIED ANAL SEX?

Some 43 percent of women say they've tried it while 19 percent say they do it occasionally. Two percent of women say they're diehard devotees of it.

FAKED AN ORGASM?

Fifty-one percent of women and 14 percent of men admit that they've pretended to climax.

THOUGHT YOUR PARTNER COULD TELL YOU FAKED IT?

Fifty-seven percent of people say they've been able to figure it out when their partners pretend. Just 32.5 percent think their partners can tell.

PARTICIPATED IN A THREESOME TO SPICE THINGS UP?

Almost two out of three people say a ménage à trois is out of the question. But 19 percent would consider it if they were unattached or if their partner approved and if the two partner options for them involved heterosexuality. Fourteen percent say they're open to whatever life has in store.

ACHIEVED ORGASM SOLELY THROUGH BREAST STIMULATION, LADIES?

Just one in one hundred women say this has happened to them.

DONE IT IN THE SNOW?

It's *brrrrr* but that hasn't dissuaded 15.5 percent of women and 11 percent of men. Of that, 10.5 percent of women and 8.4 percent of men found themselves plenty warm.

DONE IT BLINDFOLDED?

Forty-six percent of women and 40.5 percent of men have, and found it exciting. Approximately another 6 percent of each tried it but weren't all that thrilled. Forty-one percent of women and 47 percent of men have never been blindfolded or had their partner blindfolded during sex, but are open to trying it.

TRIED B&D (BONDAGE AND DISCIPLINE)?

Just over 8 percent of both men and women admit they've used a scarf, handcuffs, or rope, though most would be willing to try. Forty-five percent of women and 36 percent of men say they've considered doing it and it sounds like fun. Eight percent of women and 13 percent of men have no interest in trying.

TRIED THE SPOON POSITION?

A third of both men and men have and think it's great; another fourth of both thought it was okay. More than one in five don't know what it is.

PUT ON A STRIP SHOW FOR YOUR LOVER?

Only 41.4 percent of women and 35.4 percent of men admit they have gotten in the spirit. Two out of five of both sexes have not but are game to try it.

TRIED SPANKING?

Twenty-two percent of women have never tried it, along with 32.8 percent of men.

BEEN INTERRUPTED IN FLAGRANTE DELICTO?

Some 54 percent of women and 49 percent of men have been spared this embarrassment. On the other hand, 6 percent of women and 12 percent of men who haven't experienced this, rue the omission.

✗ WATCHED TV WHILE GOING AT IT?

Half of us shudder at the thought but 15 percent say they're into multitasking. Fourteen percent of women and 8 percent of men admit they've tried it but that it killed the mood.

KEPT A MEMENTO OF A SEXUAL CONNECTION?

A third of women and 17 percent of men still have the panties, shirt, boxers, bra, etc. from the occasion. Another 13 percent of women and 23 percent of men have kept one for a while but subsequently disposed of it.

✗ FILMED YOUR LOVEMAKING?

One in five women and 26 percent of men have played director. Most still have the tape.

✗ ACCIDENTALLY BLURTED ANOTHER'S NAME IN THE THROES OF PASSION?

Thank heavens, no, say 83 percent of women and 79 percent of men. Fifteen percent of men and women say it happened but either their partner didn't notice or it was no big deal.

✗ VISITED A NUDE BEACH OR PARK?

Seven percent of women and 11 percent of men say they have.

✗ DONE IT IN A PUBLIC PLACE?

Most men (71.2 percent) said they have. And the women were not far behind: almost 60 percent (59.4) said yes.

✗ DONE IT IN A DRESSING ROOM?

Twenty-six percent of people claim they were not daunted by in-store security cameras.

✗ ROLE-PLAYED?

Thirty-nine percent of both men and women have tried it. Just over 2 percent of us are addicted.

USED URINE IN YOUR LOVEMAKING?

Some 7 percent of people say they have peed on someone and 6 percent admit that they were peed upon. Two percent went so far as defecation.

PARTICIPATED IN A PARTNER-SWAPPING ARRANGEMENT?

Roughly 9 percent of men and women acknowledge they've played the key-swapping game. Of those, many more enjoyed the experience than complained.

SWUM IN THE NUDE?

One in five adults has shared a nude swim with 28 percent of men and 14 percent women saying so.

PLAYED STRIP POKER WITH MEN AND WOMEN?

Seems to be something from another age. Four out of five men and more than nine of every ten women profess to never having done so. Of those who did, roughly 4 percent claim it led to sex.

INVENTED A SEX TOY OUT OF A HOUSEHOLD ITEM?

One in three of us—32.8 percent—has ingeniously concocted a sex toy from something lying around the house. One in ten has played around with feathers.

STOLEN A GUY'S SHIRT AS A REMINDER?

We can only hope that guys think that a shirt is a small price to pay. Sixty-one percent of women have snatched one because they loved the way it smelled or what it represented.

BEEN SHOCKED TO FIND ASSETS YOU ADMIRED WEREN'T GENUINE?

Well over half of sexually active men admit they'd be unlikely to know if a woman's breasts were genuine or the result of a high-tech bra. Twenty-four percent say they've been disappointed or surprised on discovering the truth under the bra.

BEEN GREETED AT THE FRONT DOOR WITH A SEXY GETUP?

Forty-five percent of guys say they have been treated to this adventure, while 88 percent of men and women say they'd be happy to oblige if their partners asked. Twenty-one percent say they've surprised their mate by being nude under their coat.

USED SEX TO CURTAIL A CONVERSATION?

Thirteen percent openly admit they've had sex to put off, end, or avoid a discussion they didn't want to have.

USED SEX TO ENTICE YOUR PARTNER TO DO A CHORE?

Twelve percent openly admit to such bribery.

USED SEX TO GET OUT OF DOING SOMETHING YOU DISLIKED?

Ten percent openly admit that they've chosen the far lesser of two evils—that they have had sex to avoid something unpleasant, like going to see his folks.

INITIATED SEX TO ENTICE YOUR PARTNER TO BUY YOU SOMETHING?

Five percent consider it wise bartering.

TOLD YOUR PARTNER HE OR SHE WAS BETTER IN BED THAN HE OR SHE WAS?

Kindness reigns. Seventy percent of men and women have told their partner they were great . . . when in fact, they were middling.

FLASHED?

Fewer than 1 percent of us has.

DOWNLOADED EROTIC PICTURES FROM THE INTERNET?

Some 5.3 percent of folks admit they've downloaded the dirty.

EXCHANGED EROTIC EMAILS?

Depending on what defines erotic, 22 percent of us say we've emailed a lusty thought or two.

PAINTED A LOVER'S BODY?

Seventeen percent of women and 20 percent of men have and found it a hoot. Another 1 percent of men and women considered it a waste of time.

USED A SEX TOY OR ACCESSORY?

Twenty-seven percent of sex enthusiasts have used an erotic accessory.

INDULGED IN CROSS-DRESSING, EXHIBITIONISM, OR VOYEURISM?

Two to 5 percent of men and women say they've had one of these fetishes.

USED THE 69 POSITION IN YOUR SEXUAL ENCOUNTERS?

While 27.4 percent say they rarely if ever have sex this way, 7.2 percent claim it's their default position. Sixteen percent occasionally or more often use it. More than one in four say they have to know their partner extremely well to do this.

USED THE SIDE-BY-SIDE POSITION?

Twenty-seven percent rarely if ever do it this way. But 3.7 percent do so every time they have sex, while 16 percent do so frequently.

TRIED THE STANDING-UP POSITION?

This is even less popular than side-by-side with just 1.8 percent doing it this way every time they have sex, while 20.5 percent rarely if ever do it this way. Only 9 percent of women say it gives them a very intimate connection with their partner or ensures an orgasm.

9

Protection

WHAT FORM OF CONTRACEPTION DO YOU USE?

Some 42 million sexually active women in this country can become pregnant; 38 million of them use some form of birth control. Thirty-one percent rely on birth control pills and one in five use barrier methods. The rest use sterilization, intrauterine devices, and other techniques. Only one in four white men claim to use a rubber but 38 percent of black men and 39 percent of Latinos profess to.

HAVE YOU HAD UNPROTECTED SEX WITH A NEW PARTNER IN THE LAST YEAR?

Horrific as it may sound, 39 percent of people have, according to Durex. The condom maker found that 31 percent would still have sex, even with a partner who refused to wear a condom. Young folks are likeliest to take risks—43 percent of twenty-one to twenty-four-year-olds and 37 percent of those under sixteen have had unprotected sex with someone new in a recent twelve-month span. Men are almost twice as likely as women to throw the dice—38 percent say they'd plunge in, condom or not. Only 18 percent of women would allow that. Thirty percent of men and 41 percent of women said that a partner had tried to talk them out of using a condom.

HAVE YOU EVER FORGOTTEN TO TAKE YOUR BIRTH CONTROL PILLS?

Memory lapses are common. One in four women (24 percent) admit they've failed to take the pill at least thrice in the past year. Yet fewer than 30 percent use a condom as backup birth control.

WHAT'S THE PRIME REASON YOU USE A CONDOM?

Four out of ten people are mainly interested in preventing pregnancy but even more (50 percent) sheath up to keep themselves disease-free. Ten percent say their main focus is to keep their partner safe from disease.

WHEN DO YOU USUALLY BRING UP THE ISSUE?

Forty-two percent of guys say they initiate the conversation—or climb aboard if it's already launched—days before the actual congress. Twenty-three percent leave it until they're on the way to the bedroom. The same percent claim they don't need to discuss it as they keep a supply of condoms nearby. (Two-thirds of men store condoms within three feet of the bed. Yet 42 percent of college students claim they wanted to use a condom during sex, but didn't have one around when they needed it.) Five percent wait until the last minute, literally, just before penetration. And 2 percent broach the subject after they've already consummated the act. Four percent never mention it at all.

WHEN SHE PULLS OUT A CONDOM FROM HER PURSE, WHAT DO YOU THINK?

She's into safe sex and thank the stars, muse 62 percent. Roughly equal percents figure that she sleeps around a lot, she really wants him, or she's the kind of person who plans ahead.

HAVE YOU EVER HAD A CONDOM BREAK?

Forty-nine percent of women and 46 percent of men say it has happened causing 26.2 percent of the women and 19 percent of the men to almost have a heart attack. The Centers for Disease Control estimate that every night some 27,000 condoms break or slip on the battlefield. If you're into safety you know latex. Polyurethane condoms tear during use around 8 percent of the time versus latex condoms, which tear only 2 percent of the time.

DO YOU KNOW HOW TO PUT A CONDOM ON CORRECTLY?

For those with lots of practice it's an automatic no-brainer, and three out of five women and 90 percent of men say that applies to them. But that leaves quite a few in the dark. Four in ten don't allow ample space at the tip of the condoms, and 30 percent initially put them on upside down. Not surprisingly, 72 percent of men say they put it on themselves. The average American condom is shorter than the penises of 8 to 14 percent of guys trying to tug them on. Nearly one in three men confess they've had a condom slip off during sex.

DOES A CONDOM BOTHER YOU?

Almost a third of men admit that they lose their erection or at least some steam from putting on a condom. And two out of three women who use them experience some degree of dryness or discomfort. But the same percent don't believe that condoms significantly reduce pleasure.

IF YOU WEAR A CONDOM, WHEN DO YOU PUT IT ON . . . TAKE IT OFF?

Forty-three percent said they wore condoms during sex but didn't don them until after intercourse had begun—a no-no for those seeking to prevent pregnancy and disease. Meanwhile, 15 percent risked it all by taking them off before finishing.

HAVE YOU EVER HAD PROTECTION FAIL?

The pill fails 6.2 percent of the time and condoms 14.2 percent of the time they're worn. The diaphragm doesn't work 15.6 percent of the time and spermicide fizzes 26.3 percent of the time.

HAVE YOU EVER WORN TWO CONDOMS SIMULTANEOUSLY?

Even with knowledge of condom-failure statistics, very few men do, complaining it would be like getting a massage in a parka.

HAVE YOU EVER USED EMERGENCY OR MORNING-AFTER CONTRACEPTION?

Only 2 percent of women have ever used postcoital contraception, according to Princeton University's Office of Population Research. More than 80 percent didn't even know they could. Emergency contraception, sometimes called the "morning-after pill" can actually be taken up to three days after sex. It's different from RU-486, the European "abortion pill," which interrupts an existing pregnancy.

LADIES, ARE YOU SATISFIED WITH THE CONTRACEPTION YOU'RE USING?

Half of sexually active American women are dissatisfied with the contraception they're using for one reason or another. A big factor is that they don't always work: contraceptive failures have resulted in 1.3 million unwanted pregnancies in the U.S. each year.

HAVE YOU EVER HAD AN UNINTENDED PREGNANCY?

Almost half—48 percent—of fifteen-to-forty-four-year-old women have conceived at least once when they were not trying to. Nearly half (47 percent) of these unintended pregnancies end in abortion and 13 percent in miscarriage.

10

Fantasy Island

HOW OFTEN DO YOU CONJURE UP A FANTASY?

Men have sexual fantasies more often than women. Overall, 54 percent of men and 19 percent of women say they think about sex at least once a day. Perhaps because their minds are stretched by academics, college students are apt to think about it most with 7.2 fantasies a day for men and 4.5 for women.

WHAT ARE YOUR MOST COMMON SEXUAL FANTASIES?

Oral sex by a landslide, for both men and women. The second most common fantasy is sex with a famous person. But while men dream about multiple and interracial partners, women's fantasies more often involve sexual devices, domination, or of doing it in public places. Men are almost three times more interested in calling a phone sex line or being a porno star than women are, and they are five times likelier to want to have sex with a teenager.

DO YOU DAYDREAM ABOUT DOING IT WITH . . .

Just under three-quarters of us let our imaginations run riot about having sex with a celebrity. Half of men fantasize about sex with their best friends' partners. Some 16 percent of women think about sex with their boss. But at 7 percent, coworkers are the least likely to appear in daydreams or fantasies.

DO YOU CONJURE UP DOING IT WITH A PAST LOVER?

You bet. Almost three out of every four men and women (74 percent) concede that a former partner pops up sometimes (58 percent), if not always (16 percent) in their sexual daydreams.

HOW ABOUT DOING IT WITH YOUR BEST FRIEND? YOUR PARTNER'S SISTER?

Your best friend is out of the question for 45 percent of both men and women. The fantasizing on this front is rampant if the best friend is of a different sex. At least a quarter of men would like to do it with their partners' sisters, while more than 10 percent claimed they already had.

HAVE YOU EVER HAD A SEX FANTASY IN WHICH YOU WERE RAPING OR BEING RAPED BY SOMEONE?

More than half of women (71.9 percent) confess they've daydreamed about being forced to have sex. Only 15 percent of men and 1.5 percent of women have fantasized about forcing themselves on someone.

DO YOU IMAGINE WATCHING YOUR PARTNER DOING IT WITH SOMEONE ELSE?

This is much more uncommon. Fifty-four percent of women and 40.5 percent of men say they've never conjured up this fantasy.

DO YOU FANTASIZE ABOUT A THREESOME? TAPING IT?

Forty percent admit the thought of a two-and-one has crossed their minds. Thirty percent say they have imagined putting it on tape.

FEMMES, WHO WOULD BE THE MOST FANTASTIC FANTASY?

Forget about the girl next door, it's the boy we're after: 17.7 percent daydream about him, just about the same number musing about the hunk.

WHAT ELSE DO YOU FANTASIZE ABOUT?

Some 42 percent of men say they have fantasized about converting a lesbian. Cars figure prominently in 52 percent of love fantasies. And 41 percent of women have imagined being carted off against their will to Bali and tied to a palm tree, or some such swept-away action. Twenty-six percent fantasize about having sex in a public place.

HOW ABOUT WITH SOMEONE YOU DEFINITELY CANNOT HAVE?

Some 22 percent fantasize about sex with a forbidden lover. And 16 percent admit they daydream about sex with someone they have never met.

DO YOU FRET YOUR SEXUAL FANTASIES AREN'T "NORMAL"?

Nine percent of people worry their sexual fantasies or behaviors aren't normal. Forty-two percent of women are ashamed of at least one of them—as are 36 percent of men.

DO YOU GENERALLY SHARE YOUR FANTASIES WITH YOUR PARTNER?

Sharing it would ruin it, say 36 percent of women and 26 percent of men who keep it to themselves. Another 22 percent have something explicit in mind but are too timid to discuss. A third who spill the beans then go on to act the fantasy out, with partners under thirty-five more game on both counts. Two out of three say that it lived up to their expectations.

HAVE YOU EVER FANTASIZED ABOUT SOMEONE ELSE WHILE MAKING IT WITH YOUR MATE?

What do you mean "ever?" More than 9 percent of men and women admit they regularly do so, and 63 percent of women and 67 percent of men do so occasionally. Fifty-seven percent of women and 47.6 percent of men say they'd be bothered that their mate was fantasizing about someone else while making it with them. But 32 percent of women and 34 percent of men don't care and the rest approve and enjoy knowing about it.

GUYS, HAVE YOU EVER ADMITTED THAT YOU'VE FANTASIZED ABOUT ANOTHER WOMAN?

More than half (51 percent) of men say they have told their partner and 39 percent have even revealed who their fantasy star is.

HAVE YOU EVER TRIED TO SEDUCE SOMEONE BY CONFIDING THAT YOU'VE FANTASIZED ABOUT HIM OR HER?

Thirty-four percent of men admit trying this approach. Remarkably, only 6 percent say they've struck out with it. Even more women—39 percent—confess they've employed this technique, and only two percent say it failed to deliver.

WOULD YOU LIKE TO HAVE SEX AT LEAST ONCE A DAY?

Forty-two percent of men say they would and 25 percent of women agree.

IF YOU COULD CHANGE ONE THING ABOUT YOUR FACE TO MAKE IT SEXIER, WHAT WOULD YOU PICK?

Twenty-one percent of people wouldn't accept the offer. But 17 percent would love to alter the texture of their skin and 21 percent the whiteness or straightness of their teeth. Thirteen percent would rearrange their nose and 6 percent, reset their chin. Four percent would doctor their smile, 6 percent enlarge their eyes, and 3 percent plump up their lips.

WHAT DO YOU DREAM ABOUT MORE: RETIREMENT OR SEX?

Hitting age thirty-five seems to be a turning point: those below it dwell on sex; the daydreams of those above it migrate to retirement. While 61 percent of young guys claim to think more about sex, 62 percent of those fifty-five and older are focused on retirement.

HOW OFTEN DO YOU FANTASIZE ABOUT SEX?

Teens think about it every five minutes, according to one study, while middle-aged men (forty to forty-nine) think about it every half hour.

DO YOU THINK ABOUT SEX ON THE WAY TO WORK?

More than four out of five male commuters spend part of their journeys thinking about sex with fellow passengers. When they get to work 70 percent think about sex with their colleagues.

WHAT ARE YOU LIKELIEST TO WEAR IN A ROMANTIC FANTASY?

Surprise: it's a business suit! Thirty-six percent of people see themselves decked out thusly, compared to 22 percent wearing the uniform of a doctor or nurse, 13 percent in pilot garb, one in ten dressed as a member of the armed services, and 15 percent as a cop or firefighter. Men are twice as likely as women to fantasize about a doctor or nurse.

DO YOU WISH YOU HAD LOST YOUR VIRGINITY TO SOMEONE ELSE?

Amazingly, more than two out of every five of us (42 percent) wish they could replay the moment with someone else in the costarring role. Seventeen percent wish they'd waited longer for that big moment, while 28 percent are sorry that they waited so long.

DO YOU READ ROMANCE NOVELS AND SEE YOURSELF IN THE PAGES?

A romance novel is by one in every three bedsides in America. Some 45 percent of readers are women but 16 percent of men also tear through the pages. Readership is highest in the west and lowest in the northeast. High school graduates are the biggest fans, with readership sharply decreasing for college grads and those with less than a high school education.

WHAT'S YOUR FAVORITE LOVE STORY?

Seems *Romeo and Juliet* is synonymous with love. Even though it ends tragically, 46 percent of us think of it as the quintessential love story. Close on its heels is the pairing of Rhett Butler and Scarlett O'Hara in *Gone with the Wind*, 29 percent. Ralph and Alice Cramden from the TV show *The Honeymooners* captured 11 percent—2 percent more than *Antony and Cleopatra*.

DOES SEX IN ROMANTIC NOVELS SURPASS THE REAL THING?

You bet it does, say one in four of us (26 percent.) Forty-five percent find the real thing as powerful as what happens on the printed page and 29 percent either don't know (not having experienced one of the two) or find them equally appealing.

WHAT IS THE MOST EROTIC LOVE SCENE FOR A NON-X-RATED MOVIE?

More than a third (34 percent) say it's *9½ Weeks*. Next most heart-pounding: *Basic Instinct* with 17.3 percent of the vote. *Eyes Wide Shut* commanded 14.6 percent of the total and *Body Heat* picked up 12.4 percent of the vote, nosing out *Boogie Nights* with 12.2 percent and *Fatal Attraction* with 9.5 percent.

11

Here Comes the Bride

Each day in America roughly 6,700 couples tie the knot. Another 3,200 untie it. Ninety-five percent of us marry at some time in our lives; 60 percent are currently hitched.

WOULD YOU MARRY SOMEONE WITH ALL THE RIGHT STUFF IF YOU DIDN'T LOVE HIM OR HER?

Americans overwhelmingly say no. But Pakistanis and Indians are likely to mull it over. Some 86 percent of American college students insist they would not marry without love followed in close order by Brazilians, Mexicans, Brits, and Australians. But only 24 percent of college students in India, where arranged marriages are still common, would shun a marriage without love. Japan and the Philippines fall in between, with 62 and 64 percent saying no to marriage without love.

DID YOU LIVE TOGETHER BEFORE YOU WALKED DOWN THE AISLE?

Living together before marriage is becoming standard fare—more than a third of married couples say they gave it a trial run prior to marriage. However, two-thirds still wait until after the wedding to share living quarters.

WERE YOU ABSOLUTELY POSITIVE THIS WAS THE RIGHT MOVE?

Apparently, death, taxes, and FedEx deliveries aren't the only certainties in life. Seventy-nine percent of married folk claim they were completely certain that wearing each other's ring was the right move. Only 21 percent admitted they had second thoughts at the time (and many doubts still linger).

DO YOU EXPECT TO STAY WITH YOUR MATE UNTIL DEATH DO YOU PART?

Eighty-two percent of married men and women think that they'll stay together until death claims one of them.

DID YOU GO WITH TRADITIONAL VOWS?

Eighty-two percent of brides and grooms consummate their nuptials with classic vows. Only 4 percent write their own vows, while 13 percent add their own creative touches to traditional vows.

DID YOU TAKE (OR PLAN TO TAKE) YOUR HUSBAND'S LAST NAME?

Nine out of ten brides do. Five percent hyphenate their maiden and married names and 2 percent use their maiden name alone. Another 3 percent use an alternative such as a maiden name as middle name.

HOW OLD WERE YOU WHEN YOU (FIRST) WALKED DOWN THE AISLE?

Probably younger than first-time brides and grooms are today. The average bride nowadays weds at 24.5 years old, and the average groom at 26.7 years. Today, one in four brides is older than her husband, a far cry from 1970 when only 16 percent were. In 8 percent of marriages the woman is at least five years older. Ninety-two percent of people think there's nothing wrong with a wife being older than her husband.

IF YOU HAD THE CHANCE TO DO IT ALL AGAIN, WOULD YOU?

Only 27 percent of married couples say they wouldn't. And 30 percent of those married six to nine years have wished they could wake up and find themselves single. Fifteen percent would postpone their wedding a tad so they could be more financially independent or academically advanced. But they'd still stay with the same partner.

ASSUMING YOU'RE IN A GOOD MARRIAGE, WAS YOUR WEDDING DAY YOUR HAPPIEST EVER?

It was if you haven't experienced childbirth. Fifty-three percent of husbands and wives claim the day their child was born tickled them pink (or blue) more than any other occasion, while 32 percent say their happiest moment was when they said I do. Eight percent were happiest on graduation from high school or college and 3 percent when a divorce became final. Two percent say their most joyous moment was receiving a big job promotion.

WAS YOUR WEDDING DAY THE EVENT YOU MOST LOOKED FORWARD TO, LADIES?

It's in second place, trailing just behind the day their partner proposed. But 85 percent considered the proposal they received was less romantic than they had anticipated or hoped for. Four out of five would never tell their boyfriends what they did wrong.

WHAT MONTH DID YOU WALK DOWN THE AISLE?

If the past is any prelude to the future, more people will marry in June and August than at any other time of the year. Eleven percent of marriages take place in those two months. September and July are the next most popular and January the least. Only slightly more appealing: February and March.

WHAT TIME OF DAY DID YOU TIE THE KNOT?
Sixty percent of weddings take place in the afternoon, while 25 percent prefer evening weddings, and 15 percent favor morning weddings.

HAVE YOU BEEN HERE BEFORE?
It's déjà vu for at least one member of the happy couple in 46 percent of marriages. Four in ten remarriages unite two divorced persons, while half of them were a first marriage for one member of the couple. These were evenly split between remarrying brides and remarrying grooms. In 11 percent of remarriages, one or both members of the couples were widowed. The average divorced woman who gets remarried is thirty-five years old and has been divorced for 3.9 years. The average divorced man is thirty-nine and has waited 3.6 years.

HOW LONG DID YOU PLAN YOUR WEDDING?
You could have built the New York City subway system. Thirty percent say they pored over plans for seven to twelve months and 14 percent say they've been at it for twelve to eighteen months. Only 27 percent pulled it off within three months. Twenty-six percent devoted four to six months to arrangements. Four percent say they've worked on it for more than two years. The average bride spends eight hours a week on wedding plans. Almost half (48 percent) wish they could take a leave of absence from work to plan the wedding full-time. Five percent fret about being so distracted by the wedding that they might get fired or flunk out of school. Only 12 percent of Americans consulted a professional wedding planner.

DID YOU DO ANY LAST MINUTE NIP AND TUCKS?
Thirty-seven percent of brides go in for a body part fix-up before the big day. Most common adjustments: teeth whitening, dermatology, breast implants, tummy tucks, laser surgery, and tattoo removal. Fifty-four percent revved up their diet and exercise regimens to get in shape for the occasion.

WHAT, ME WORRIED?

More than three out of four brides-to-be feel overwhelmed by last-minute details (77 percent). Two-thirds (66 percent) worry they can't afford their ideal honeymoon and 59 percent that they've offended people they left off the invitation list.

HEY BRIDES, WHAT'S THE MOST DIFFICULT ASPECT OF PLANNING YOUR WEDDING?

It's pulling together the wedding budget and sticking to it that's a struggle for 41 percent of those soon to walk the plank. Another 30 percent have trouble finding time to make all the phone calls, fittings, trips to vendors, and staying organized. Twenty-eight percent of brides find dealing with so many different vendors harder than dealing with family disagreements (13 percent) over the wedding plans.

HOW STRESSFUL IS PLANNING A WEDDING?

Seventeen percent confess they'd be more upset about losing their wedding planners than their wallets. One in four (24 percent) admit feeling anxious about the wedding plans every day since they got engaged. Only 22 percent are almost never stressed about the wedding.

BRIDES, DID YOU WANT THE GROOM'S HELP PLANNING THE BIG DAY?

Not always: 16 percent of brides secretly wish that their fiancés would butt out of the wedding planning.

DID PLANNING THE WEDDING INTERFERE WITH THE TIME YOU SPENT AS A COUPLE?

It did for 31 percent of people—meaning 17 percent spent less time together and 14 percent spent more. The quality of time has also been eroded for 36 percent who've had more fights than ever, but 28 percent say the process has brought them closer together. The rest say it hasn't hurt or helped their relationship at all.

WHAT DID YOU ARGUE ABOUT MOST WITH YOUR PARTNER WHILE PLANNING YOUR WEDDING?

For 25 percent, the biggest hot spot was money and how to allocate it, while another 24 percent were steamed that their partners weren't pulling their weight. Nineteen percent claimed not to have argued at all, while 16 percent got testy with each other over in-law issues and 13 percent over the guest list. Six percent say *everything* stressed them and provoked arguments.

DO YOU THINK IT'S BAD LUCK FOR THE GROOM TO SEE THE BRIDE RIGHT BEFORE THE CEREMONY?

Twenty-four percent of superstitious folks would rather not take the chance.

HOW LONG DOES THE TYPICAL ENGAGEMENT LAST?

Sixteen months, up from eleven months in 1990.

HOW DID YOU KEEP THE FLAME BURNING DURING HIGH-STRESS TIMES?

The most popular strategy was conscientious "making up" when the fight was over, practiced by 44 percent of those betrothed. Another 37 percent planned special dates to smooth over the rough patches, while 13 percent resorted to love notes and 6 percent to romantic getaways.

HOW MANY GUESTS DID YOU HAVE AT THE WEDDING?

In a recent year the average wedding had 171 guests, although 53 percent of couples claim they'd have preferred to have fewer than one hundred. Just 7 percent want to invite the town (more than two hundred and fifty guests), although eighteen- to twenty-four-year-olds were the most likely to want a big wedding (14 percent).

HOW MUCH DID THE WEDDING SET YOU BACK?

A first-time wedding in a recent year averaged $22,360. The lion's share of that went for the reception venue and food ($7,246). An average second wedding runs $12,000. Almost a third of all marriages today are second-timers. The average age for women to remarry is thirty-six and men, thirty-nine.

WHO PAID?
More than one in four couples (27 percent) paid their own way. The bride's parents pick up the whole tab just 19 percent of the time. A bride's second wedding is usually paid for by the couple, not the parents.

DID YOU TOSS YOUR GARTER?
Four out of five brides have tossed their garters.

DID YOU WEAR SOMETHING OLD, SOMETHING NEW, SOMETHING BORROWED, AND SOMETHING BLUE?
Eighty-nine percent of brides say they've tried to honor this tradition.

DID DAD WALK YOU DOWN THE AISLE?
In 78 percent of recent marriages, the bride has walked down the aisle accompanied by Daddy.

DID YOU CRY AT YOUR OWN WEDDING?
One in four grooms admit they weep, and 45 percent of brides concede they've shed a tear or two at their own wedding.

DID YOU LIKE YOUR WEDDING PHOTOS?
Not much, say most. Over a quarter of newlyweds didn't like *any* of their official pictures at all and selected informal shots taken by friends for framing instead. Three-quarters of brides wished they could change the photos (most wanting to look slimmer). Just one in one-hundred wedding photos taken wind up in the album, and one in five-hundred makes it onto the wall or mantelpiece. The photography or videography at an average wedding cost $1,263. Women are too discreet to admit it but one in ten men would doctor their wedding pictures to digitally remove their mothers-in-law, or some other unwelcome creature, if they could get away with it.

DO YOU WEAR YOUR WEDDING RING?
Perhaps because it's a don't-fence-me-in expression but 14 percent of people who claim to be happily married don't wear a wedding band.

HOW MUCH DID YOU SPEND ON A WEDDING GOWN?

In a recent year the average wedding dress costs $949. Sixty percent of brides spent less than $750, while 18 percent spent between $750 and $1,000. Another 14 percent shelled out between $1,000 to $2,000 for that special dress and 8 percent splurged, spending $2,000 or more on a gown. Some 99 percent of grooms wear formal attire at an average cost of $77 for a rental.

HOW MANY WEDDING GOWNS DID YOU TRY ON?

The average bride tried on a dozen dresses before selecting the winner. One in five sampled more than twenty-one gowns before choosing the right one; and an equal number cried when they found it.

WAS YOUR WEDDING DRESS SATIN? SIMPLE? WHITE?

Floor-length gowns are worn by 89 percent of first-time brides. Fifty-six percent were satin and 46 percent were straight and simple. Thirty-one percent opted for a strapless, sexy look. One in five (19 percent) chose the full and fancy look, while 4 percent kept it classic, with long sleeves and lace. Some 94.6 percent of first-time brides wear white or off-white. Almost nine out of ten brides in first-time weddings wear a veil even though it's a symbol of virginity and nine out of ten second-time brides opt instead for a hat or a wreath of fresh flowers.

WHAT'S YOUR FAVORITE WEDDING FLOWER?

A rose by any other name should still sweeten a wedding. Seventy-two percent of Americans pick roses as part of their weddings, with carnations as the second choice (40 percent). Thirty-four percent opt for lilies, 23 percent for daisies, and 19 percent for tulips.

WHAT'S YOUR FAVORITE WEDDING SONG?

"At Last" (Etta James) took the cake followed by "From This Moment On" (Shania Twain) and "Amazed" (Lonestar) in a recent year. On the other hand, more people would like "The Chicken Dance Song" forever banned from weddings than any other song, followed by "The Macarena" (Los del Rio) and "My Heart Will Go On" (Celine Dion).

WHAT'S THE MOST ROMANTIC WEDDING GESTURE?

Half say it's the first dance by the bride and groom; 32 percent feel it's writing special marriage vows; and 18 percent regard the feeding of the wedding cake to each other as symbolic of the romantic union.

DID YOU PROPOSE (OR WERE YOU PROPOSED TO) ON BENDED KNEE?

Seems kneeling has gone out of style. Fewer than one in five of us has proposed, or been proposed to, on bended knee.

WHO DID THE PROPOSING?

In nearly one in ten of all marriage proposals today, it's the women who are in charge.

DID YOU PROPOSE ON THE PHONE?

Six percent of marriage proposals are delivered over the phone.

DID YOU SEEK PARENTAL APPROVAL?

Just 4 percent of grooms have asked the fathers of the bride for "permission" to marry their daughters.

DID YOU SWEAT OVER THE PROPOSAL?

For 41 percent of guys, the biggest worry about proposing is the fear of rejection. One in four are traumatized by finding the right words. Eleven percent are nervous about the pressure to be perfect and 9 percent are flummoxed over the cost of the ring.

WHEN DID YOU POP THE QUESTION?

"Rudolph the Red-Nosed Reindeer" seems to be more of a matrimonial motivator than "My Funny Valentine." Thirteen percent of proposals are made around Christmastime versus 8 percent on or around Valentine's Day.

HAVE YOU EVER TURNED DOWN A MARRIAGE PROPOSAL—OR HAD ONE TURNED DOWN?

One in seventeen marriage proposals have been rejected.

DID YOU (OR WILL YOU) TAKE A HONEYMOON?

Most newlyweds do. The average honeymoon lasts nine days and costs $3,657. The most popular sites are the Caribbean (27 percent), Hawaii (18 percent), Bahamas (9 percent), and Europe (8 percent).

DID YOU *NOT* DO IT ON YOUR WEDDING NIGHT?

Twenty-eight percent of married couples didn't have sex on their wedding night, mostly because they were too tired. But 12 percent opted to hang out with their friends instead, while 5 percent admit they were too drunk to perform. Most couples, however, make up for it by making love an average 2.28 times a day during the honeymoon. Twenty-five percent did it at least three times on their wedding night.

HOW LONG IS THE HONEYMOON?

For 56 percent of couples one week is the deal, while 25 percent extend it longer. Fifteen percent plan to take four to six days and 4 percent nip out for between one and three days.

WHO PAYS FOR THE HONEYMOON?

Sixty-three percent say the honeymoon will be the costliest trip they've taken to date as an adult. Nearly half will use wedding-gift money to help fund the trip.

WHAT WOULD BE THE WORST FAUX PAS A GUY COULD MAKE ON HIS HONEYMOON?

Calling Mom (12 percent) may be the wrong move but it pales in comparison to bringing a laptop computer along (23 percent). That offense even tops declining sex (22 percent), and looking attentively at a member of the opposite sex, which is tied with watching sports on TV (16 percent).

DID YOU MUSE ABOUT YOUR PARTNER OR OTHER HONEYMOONERS?

Hate to say it, but, um, yeah admit one in three guys.

DID YOU CARRY YOUR BRIDE (OR WERE YOU CARRIED) OVER THE THRESHOLD?

Thirty-nine percent of men say they've actually carried their brides over the threshold to honor the tradition.

HOW MUCH DID YOU SPEND ON AN ENGAGEMENT RING?

In a recent year the average engagement ring costs $2,982. Brides wear their engagement rings for approximately 11.5 months before they add on a wedding band. Assuming it's a surprise, seven out of ten men say they shop for the ring alone.

WOULD YOU BUY A CUBIC ZIRCONIA RING IF YOU COULD GET AWAY WITH IT?

One in eleven guys would.

GUYS, WHAT'S YOUR FIRST DESTINATION CHOICE FOR A BACHELOR PARTY?

Las Vegas wins with gambling (38 percent) and golf (31 percent) listed as the top activities. But seven out of ten men admit they were bored by their bachelor parties.

WHAT BUGS WOMEN MOST ABOUT BACHELOR PARTIES?

It's not the trust issue as much as disappointment that their fiancés would *want* to join in such bacchanalias. And they feel threatened by what their honeys' *friends* might have in store for him that night. The average guy's bachelor party costs $1,000 and includes ten attendees who down four cases of beer. There's a one in three probability of seeing a stripper.

HAVE YOU HEARD THE WEDDING MARCH THIS YEAR?

Some 42 percent of adults have attended a wedding during the past year that was not their own. While 87 percent of us think love for another person can last a lifetime, almost two of every three people (64 percent) attending any given wedding think that the coupling will end in divorce.

DO YOU THINK A PRENUP MAKES SENSE?

Twenty-eight percent consider a prenup a savvy financial move but only one in four think it really only makes sense for the rich and famous. Fifteen percent feel it dooms a marriage to fail.

WOULD YOU SIGN A PRENUP?

Two out of three women (68 percent) and 63 percent of men won't sign one, according to Prudential. But just 36 percent overall say they'd outright refuse if their partner requested it.

HAVE YOU TOSSED RICE?

Forty-one percent of wedding guests say they've honored the bride and groom by tossing birdseed or rice at them. Fifteen percent have blown bubbles or in some other way joyously sent off the newly-weds.

DO YOU USUALLY GIVE THE BRIDE AND GROOM MATRI-MONEY?

You can be fairly sure they want it, although it probably won't show up on the Williams-Sonoma gift registry. Ninety-four percent of engaged couples admit they'd be tickled to open a gift that says "Pay to the Order of. . . ." Just about one of every ten traditional wedding gifts goes back to the store, often to pay wedding expenses. Most newlyweds start their marriages in debt.

OTHER THAN DOUGH, WHAT DO NEWLYWEDS WANT AS A GIFT?

Money wins hands down, but 21 percent would also appreciate furniture (21 percent), cooking equipment (19 percent), and china (11 percent). Five percent want nontraditional stuff like trips and camping gear.

WHAT DO YOU USUALLY SPEND ON A WEDDING GIFT?

Two out of three about-to-be-marrieds expect their wedding guests to spend between fifty and a hundred dollars on a gift. Eighteen percent count on guests to spend fifty or less, while 15 percent expect bigger things, like $100–$200 gifts. Just 1.5 percent expect gifts worth over $200.

DID YOU REGISTER? WHEN?

Nearly all about-to-be couples register and more than half do it online. Most register at several places: 41 percent at two locations and 37 percent at three. Only 10 percent registered in a sole location. Two-thirds of newlyweds registered six months before the nuptials. Nearly one in five signed up before the engagement party (generally six weeks after the proposal), and 17 percent selected what they wanted three months before. Just 2 percent registered less than one month before marriage.

HAVE YOU EVER BEEN LEFT AT THE ALTAR . . . OR KNOW SOMEONE WHO HAS BEEN?

A surprising one in ten of us admit that they have been left at the altar or know a friend who has. More men (11 percent) than women (7 percent) report having been stood up on their wedding day.

DID YOU EVER WISH YOU'D JUST ELOPED?

Fifty percent of TBW (traditional big wedding) veterans wished they'd gone off by themselves and privately taken their vows. But not a single eloper wished he or she had done a big traditional wedding.

12

Cheating and Morality

Four in ten people would try to pad an insurance bill to cover the deductible, and one in three has intentionally walked out of a store without paying for something. Surely ethical breaches have spilled over into our most important relationships, or have they?

In 1953, renowned sex researcher Alfred Kinsey found that half of American husbands and 26 percent of wives had cheated by the time they turned forty. A 1997 Ball State University study found that women under forty, are just as likely to commit adultery as men their age. What's going on?

HAVE YOU EVER HAD AN AFFAIR?

The numbers are all over the place. Today, at least one in three of us has had, or is having, an extramarital affair. Fewer than 1 percent of marrieds have had multiple affairs. The average affair lasts almost a year. For most it's not a matter of love but lust. Two-thirds of men and 57 percent of women involved outside their prime relationships declare they don't love their sex partner. But most women like the sex with their lovers more than what they're getting at home; men feel the other way.

WHO DID YOU HAVE AN AFFAIR WITH?

Most of these interactions are with longtime friends (57 percent) of at least six months. Nine percent are with colleagues.

WHAT MOTIVATES AN AFFAIR?

While a few men get involved in affairs to avoid getting too close to their wives, most are simply succumbing to temptation or the desire to want to massage their egos. Women, on the other hand, tend to cheat for emotional or financial support, they want nurturing, reinforcement of their own desirability, or money and other material perks the sex can provide. Others (both men and women) are lonely, bored by monotonous marriages, vengeful after finding telltale signs of their partners' infidelity, or lured by sexual excitement. When women cheat it's often when the marriage is in trouble.

IF YOU HAD AN AFFAIR WOULD YOU TELL YOUR PARTNER ABOUT IT?

Surveys from the 1960s suggest that fewer than half of cheating husbands told their wives. More recently, 43 percent say they'd feel terrible and compelled to tell their mate. But 49 percent admit that while they'd feel bad, they wouldn't spill the beans so as not to hurt their partners. Another 8 percent would keep mum but wouldn't feel any conscience twinges. Amazingly, 62 percent think there's nothing wrong with an outside fling.

IF YOUR PARTNER CHEATED, WOULD YOU WANT A CONFESSION?

You bet, say 72 percent who feel they deserve to know. The rest believe that no good could come from this declaration, that they'd want their partner to keep it quiet and not let it happen again.

EVER HAD A ONE-NIGHT STAND?

Sixty percent of men and 54 percent of women have had at least one, one-night stand. One in five men and one in ten women admit they've had more than a few. And while four out of five women think one-night stands are morally wrong, only 60 percent of men feel the same way.

HOW DID YOU FEEL THE NEXT MORNING?

The overriding sensation for women was guilt (28 percent), while another 18 percent claim they felt more used than they had anticipated. Seventeen percent felt naughty—about the same number who felt refreshed or exhilarated. It's no great shakes for men either. Just 43 percent felt rejuvenated or exhilarated, while 20 percent felt naughty. Eight percent of men admitted they felt used.

IF YOU HAVEN'T HAD AN AFFAIR, DO YOU THINK ABOUT IT?

From time to time the thought ambushes slightly more than half of us, but only 21 percent admit they do contemplate the idea often.

IF YOU FOUND YOUR PARTNER CHEATING, WHAT WOULD YOU DO?

Walk out the door, say 40 percent. Another 29 percent, reluctant to end their relationships, would discuss the matter and try everything else to solve the issue. One in four can't surmise what they'd do and don't want to try, while 3.4 percent would push it to the back of their minds and try to not think about it. Just over 2 percent say it would not pose a problem. Twenty-two percent say an eye for an eye—if their partner was cheating, they'd see that as an invitation to cheat back.

WHAT WOULD HEIGHTEN THE CHANCES YOU'D CHEAT?

For 12 percent, if they knew they could cheat and not get caught, they'd plow ahead. Nine percent say they'd be likelier to cheat on their partners if they could sleep with a celebrity. After all, star*fucking* doesn't really count as cheating anyway. Just 4 percent would find fighting and not getting along as a motivation to begin an affair.

DO YOU EXPECT FAITHFULNESS OVER A LONG SEPARATION?

Obviously that depends on the nature of the relationship and the separation. Marrieds overwhelmingly expect fidelity, but one in three college students admits to being unfaithful to his or her partner back home while at university.

WOULD YOU SEEK PROFESSIONAL HELP FOR INFIDELITY?

Americans believe spousal unfaithfulness is second only to physical violence in the harm it does to the cheated partner. Yet if a friend asks for advice about coping with an unfaithful spouse, fewer than half (45 percent) would suggest seeking professional help. At the same time 76 percent would urge their friends to seek professional help for depression, 67 percent for a child out of control, and 63 percent for impotence.

WHAT WOULD YOU DO IF A PARTNER'S FRIEND MADE A PASS AT YOU?

Even if the candidate were a ten, one in five people would reject the pursuant, then confide the overture to their partner. Fifty-four percent would tell him or her no and drop it there. Another 22 percent would rebuff that particular advance but make it clear the door could open in the future and 4 percent would go for it.

IS FLIRTING CHEATING?

Some people have very loose definitions of what constitutes cheating. A third of married men and 38 percent of married women think flirting is cheating. Four out of ten married men and half of women view holding hands with someone else as deceitful. Some 59 percent of married men and 75 percent of married women think kissing someone else counts as cheating. And 64 percent of married men and 72 percent of women put sexually explicit phone chats in this column.

WHAT ABOUT PLATONIC LOVE OR FRIENDSHIP?

Even if no overt action is taken, you're still guilty. Sixty percent of men and 64 percent of women categorize falling in love with another, even without any physical intimacy whatsoever, to be cheating. And 30 percent of women and 24 percent of men consider having a close friend of the opposite sex and not telling their spouse about it to be cheating.

HOW ABOUT FANTASIZING ABOUT HAVING SEX WITH SOMEONE ELSE?

You shall not lust even in your heart say 39 percent of married men and 43 percent of married women.

HOW ABOUT ORAL SEX, WITHOUT PENETRATION?

Just 10 percent of women and 17.5 percent of men *don't* think that constitutes infidelity.

IS AN INTERNET ROMANCE CHEATING?

Nearly three of four adults (65 percent of men and 75 percent of women) say that a cyber affair counts as a real one, and if done in tandem with a physical one, constitutes betrayal.

DO YOU THINK IT'S WORSE FOR A HUSBAND OR A WIFE TO CHEAT?

Although in some cultures it's more acceptable for men to be unfaithful to their wives, Americans don't buy that. Seventy-eight percent don't think it's worse for a wife to cheat. At the same time, 9 percent consider that a more heinous crime.

WHAT CLUED YOU IN THAT YOUR PARTNER WAS CHEATING?

When their guy dispensed with a kiss on the cheek before leaving for work in the morning, it was a likely sign he was doing his kissing elsewhere, said 61 percent of women. Half suspected something was up when their slovenly mate suddenly spruced himself up and took new pride in his appearance. Slightly fewer (47 percent) began to piece things together when their partner no longer wanted to talk about plans for the future, suggesting he had other plans. Alarm bells went off for a third of women when their mates stopped initiating sex. The rest figured that's not unusual in a long-term relationship.

HAVE YOU EVER FOLLOWED UP ON THOSE CLUES YOURSELF?

One in ten admits calling to check that their partners are where they said they would be. Two out of three admit to snooping on their partners' phone calls or going through their partners' mobile phone inbox to read their text messages. A third of men and 27 percent of women admit that they have searched through their partners' pants or purse, looking for incriminating evidence. Three percent went as far as hiring a private detective.

HAVE YOU EVER RUN A PERSONAL AD WHEN YOU WERE ALREADY MARRIED?

Thirty-five percent of people who use personal ads for dating are already married.

HAVE YOU EVER CHECKED INTO A HOTEL UNDER A BOGUS NAME?

One in three couples have checked into a hotel or guesthouse under bogus names.

HAVE YOU EVER LIED TO A PROSPECTIVE PARTNER TO SEAL THE DEAL?

We probably lie about out age and weight more than anything else but a third of men and one in ten women own up to altering the truth in order to pave the path to sex. Almost half of men and 42 percent of women acknowledge that they've fibbed about the number of previous sexual partners, overstating *and* understating them about equally, to ingratiate themselves. Twenty-three percent of men and 10 percent of women avow they'd conceal having another current partner if they were two-timing.

HAVE YOU EVER BOASTED ABOUT DOING EXTREME SPORTS TO PIQUE A PROSPECT'S INTEREST?

Guys and gals see members of the opposite sex who go on adventure holidays or indulge in such activities as white-water rafting as exciting, cultured, interesting—and more attractive. Twelve percent of folks admit they've embellished their achievements in arenas like these to get to first base.

HAVE YOU EVER USED FORCE OR EXPLOITATION TO GET SEX?

Date rape is a lot more common than anyone thought. Two out of three middle-class nineteen-year-old men had gotten a date drunk. Two out of five had used verbal intimidation and almost one in five had used force or threats. Fifty-eight percent of university coeds say that while they may not have called it rape, they have experienced intercourse against their will.

IF YOU WANTED A BABY AND YOUR PARTNER DIDN'T, WOULD YOU ENGINEER IT?

Almost one in four women would try to conceive without their partners' consent if they wanted a baby.

IF YOU LEARNED YOU WERE HIV POSITIVE, WOULD YOU TELL YOUR PARTNER?

Twelve percent of men would not share the dire news with their lover.

HAVE YOU EVER HAD SEX WITH A MINOR?

Four out of ten people have, but most of them were themselves minors at the time.

HAVE YOU EVER HAD SEX WITH A COUSIN?

This is edging close to *Deliverance* territory but 8 percent confess it's true. Six percent even admit to doing the deed with a sibling or half-sibling.

HAVE YOU EVER MISREPRESENTED YOURSELF IN A CHAT ROOM?

One of every four web users has adopted a new identity in cyberland. Nineteen percent of aliases pretended to be female and 10 percent masqueraded as male. One in four misrepresentations position their senders as considerably thinner than they are, and one in ten lied about his or her age.

HAVE YOU EVER SENT A SEXY SELF-PORTRAIT ONLINE?

What's the hitch there, wonder 28 percent of us who've e-photoed. Eight percent have even sent someone a picture of themselves naked. And 7 percent have sent out a naked picture of someone else claiming it was a self-portrait!

HAVE YOU EVER DOWNLOADED PORN?

Almost half of us (45 percent) admit to saving for later perusal something that tickled our fancy. Seventy-five percent say it's okay with their partners if they visit an adult website.

IS IT OKAY TO GIVE YOUR PHONE NUMBER TO SOMEONE YOU MET ONLINE?

No way, say four out of five of us. But the same percent think it's perfectly acceptable to have an instant message chat with someone of the opposite sex whom they don't know.

HAVE YOU EVER PAID FOR SEX?

While virtually all of us have in one way or another paid for sex (without actually shelling out money), 11 percent of folks have paid cash or put it on their credit cards. Six percent say they were payees. But fewer than 7 percent have lost their virginity to a prostitute. Prostitutes say their main request is for oral sex. Amazingly, 11 percent of men and 4 percent of women don't consider prostitution to be cheating. They figure that if money changes hands it doesn't count.

WOULD YOU HAVE SEX FOR CASH?

Two out of three men would consider this a worthy proposition. Sixteen percent would do it for $150 or less. A quarter of men require at least $1,500, and 35 percent would want ten times that. Fifty-one percent would sell their bod for $150,000. Women put a higher price on the transaction. Only 3 percent would do it for $150, 8 percent for $1,500, 16 percent for $15,000, and 29 percent for $150,000.

HAVE YOU EVER HAD SEX WITH A FRIEND'S LOVER BEHIND THEIR BACK?

Fourteen percent grant that they furtively have dated or slept with a friend's partner without their friend's knowledge.

WOULD YOU TELL A FRIEND IF YOU KNEW HIS OR HER SPOUSE WAS CHEATING ON HIM OR HER?

Even if the bearer of bad news gets blamed, 60 percent of people say they would let a friend know. Women are more than twice as likely as men to honor this perceived responsibility of friendship. Sixteen percent of men and women would mind their own business.

IS IT A SIN TO "LIVE IN SIN"?

The majority of us believe it's a good idea to live together before taking the plunge. But nearly half say there's no reason then to marry.

DO YOU FURTIVELY DISAPPROVE OF GAYS?

They probably do not want to admit it but 42 percent of Americans disapprove of homosexuality. That's twice the number of Brits who do. Sixteen percent of Italians cluck their tongues as do 15 percent of French, 9 percent of Dutch, and 5 percent of Spaniards.

WOULD YOU HAVE SEX WITH A PROFESSOR IF IT GUARANTEED AN "A"?

Almost half (47 percent) of college students say they would sleep their way to a good grade if it was a sure thing and came without any reprisal.

HAVE YOU EVER SAID "I LOVE YOU" WHEN IT WASN'T TRUE?

Turns out that 44 percent of us have committed this particular fib.

CAN YOU LIE TO YOUR PARTNER WITHOUT THEM KNOWING?

Thirty percent of men and 65 percent of women say that they can and that they have! While 89 percent of people believe that mutual trust is very important in a relationship, only 69 percent trust their mate completely. Four percent contend they don't trust their partner at all.

13

Other Dark Corners

A decade ago, the most common sexual dysfunctions were premature ejaculation and the inability to reach orgasm. Today those are still common, but so are so-called desire disorders, with both men and women wanting more than they can get. Overall, 43 percent of women and 31 percent of men claim to have persistent problems with sex.

ARE YOU FRUSTRATED BY FOREPLAY?
The average guy spends fifteen minutes on foreplay irking 34 percent of his partners who grumble that he's rushing things. Yet another 4 percent who want to get it over with complain that foreplay lasts too long!

WHAT ELSE ARE YOU WANTING?
Sixty percent of men and women yearn for more variety in their lovemaking and 51 percent of women and two-thirds of men crave more oral sex. Thirty percent would love to hear some praise or words of endearment from their partner during copulation, as well as before and after.

HAVE YOU EVER FELT FORCED INTO AN UNWANTED SEXUAL SITUATION?

Twelve percent of young women have been bullied into going further than they felt comfortable at least once. And the National Adolescent Student Health Survey found that nearly one in five girls felt pressured to have sex during the past year.

HAVE YOU EVER BEEN RAPED?

Rape may be the most common violent crime. One in every six American women has at one time or another been the victim: 14.8 percent of completed rape and 2.8 percent of attempted rape. So have 3 percent of men. Almost half of all rape victims are under eighteen. Three in five knew their assailant, but 72 percent never reported the rape to the police figuring it would be pointless. They may be right; an arrest is made only half the time a rape is reported. Of that, 20 percent don't get prosecuted. Among prosecuted cases there's a 58 percent chance of a felony conviction—and then only a 69 percent chance the rapist will spend time in jail. Yet 62 percent of women and 44 percent of men say they'd turn in a "friend" who raped them to the police.

HAVE YOU EVER ENDURED SEX YOU DESPISED FOR A LONG TIME?

While "long time" is a relative term, two out of five women say they have gritted their teeth and put up with it either because it was the path of least resistance or they didn't feel they had a choice.

DO YOU REALLY NOT ENJOY IT MOST OF THE TIME?

Thirty-one percent of women admit they could take it or leave it, and 21 percent would rather leave it; they don't enjoy it all. Fourteen percent say it hurts. Twenty-six percent complain they regularly don't reach orgasm. As for men, 14 percent of them aren't interested either, including 8 percent who find it unpleasant.

HAVE YOU EVER HAD TROUBLE HOLDING THOSE HORSES?

Rein it in, big boy. Between 15 to 20 percent of men—especially young ones—can't control when they come. Nearly one in three couples consider premature ejaculation a problem that at least occasionally erupts between their sheets.

HAVE YOU TRIED TO GET PREGNANT AND FAILED?

Infertility sneaks up on you along with wrinkles and sags. One in ten couples suffers from it. The average couple in their twenties conceives within five months of trying and 86 percent, within a year. By the time the woman is thirty-five, the success rate drops to 52 percent over twelve months and it keeps dropping as she keeps aging. By the time the participants are forty, they're batting 35 percent and by age forty-five, it's less than five percent. Half of all couples over age thirty-seven grapple with infertility and by age forty-two, nine in ten will. Half the time it's a question of female plumbing; 30 percent of the time it's the man's sperm count, shape, or motility. In one in five cases both the man and woman contribute.

HAS SNORING PUT A DAMPER ON YOUR SEX LIFE?

"Damper?" Call this the kibosh. One in four cohabiting couples snort that their sex life has been ruined by snoring.

HOW ABOUT HEARTBURN?

In medical terms it's called acid reflux; in sexual terms it's a big red stop sign for a third of us.

ARE YOU JUST TOO TIRED?

Despite all the banter about headaches, it's fatigue that is the main excuse for not having sex, with worries about disturbing the wee ones a close runner-up rationale for many women.

ARE YOU AFFECTED BY PMS, LADIES?

Moodiness, irritability, mood swings, headaches, weight gain, fatigue, food cravings: these are the calling cards of premenstrual syndrome and 85 percent of women report experiencing one or more of these symptoms. For 10 percent the assault is debilitating, and their interest in sex shrivels.

IF YOU'VE GOT A SEX PROBLEM, WITH WHOM DO YOU DISCUSS IT?

If sex is hard to talk about, a sexual problem is close to impossible. For those who discuss it at all, 56 percent confide in their doctors and 16 percent share it with their mates. Ten percent talk to a friend and 2 percent to a relative.

HAVE YOU EVER GONE LIMP WHEN IT MATTERED?

That depends a lot on how old you are. Collectively, guys stand a one in three chance of having their member balk but the likelihood of so-called erectile dysfunction increases by 300 percent after age fifty.

HAVE YOU EVER HAD TROUBLE GETTING IT UP?

Which is worse, having it go limp or not being able to raise the flag at all? Apparently, a third of forty- to seventy-year-old men have significant erectile dysfunction.

HAVE YOU DONE ANYTHING ABOUT IT?

Historically, only one in five men has ever sought help but now more than 20 million men around the world use the diamond-shaped blue pill or one of the clones regularly. In the U.S. one in every five men over age forty has tried Viagra and, on average, nine Viagra pills are dispensed every second. About half of patients who ask their doctors for a prescription are forty to fifty-nine years old.

DID IT WORK?

Eighty-three percent of those who've tried Viagra for a few weeks have scored at least once, boasts Pfizer, which makes the drug. The company claims the average erection lasts a minute with 100 mg of Viagra compared to 3.6 seconds with a placebo. But 23 percent who took that dose suffered headaches, 17 percent got red-faced, 12 percent had tummyaches, 3 percent had vision problems, nasal congestion, and urinary tract infections, and 2 percent developed rashes.

DID YOU REFILL THE VIAGRA PRESCRIPTION?

Half of those who try Viagra abandon ship before the recommended eight doses. Pfizer says they give up because of other issues not related to how well the drug works.

HAVE YOU SOUGHT HELP FOR A LOW SEX DRIVE?

Few even want to admit it's a problem. The U.S. Food and Drug Administration estimates that 4 to 5 million men suffer from low testosterone, but only 5 percent seek treatment. Only half of guys with diminished sex drive concede they might contact a doctor for help. Only a third of women expected their men would.

HAVE YOU EVER HAD A SEXUALLY TRANSMITTED DISEASE?

In the U.S. more than 12 million new cases occur each year. Just about one in every six adults has had one. Two-thirds of all STDs occur in adolescents and young adults.

HAVE YOU EVER HAD CHLAMYDIA?

Chances are, yes. Four of the ten most reported diseases are STDs: chlamydial infection, gonorrhea, AIDS, and syphilis. But *Chlamydia trachomatis* is the most common, striking four million women annually, at least half of whom have no symptoms.

WHAT DO YOU KNOW ABOUT HPV?

You probably know HPV as genital warts but you probably didn't know that in the U.S. twenty-four million people are infected with the virus. Over a million new infections of human papillomavirus occur each year with warts ranging from as big as nickels to too tiny to see.

HAVE YOU EVER HAD GENITAL HERPES?

You just might have and didn't know it. More than half of the 45 million Americans in this country infected with the virus that causes genital herpes (just about one in five people) don't know they have it. More than five hundred thousand new cases are diagnosed each year. One out of every four or five pregnant women has it but fewer than a tenth of 1 percent of them pass it on to their babies. The average person has four to five outbreaks a year. The first one often packs the biggest wallop and attacks decline in severity and frequency over time. And experts estimate that 50 to 80 percent of Americans have oral herpes.

ARE YOU SEXUALLY OBSESSED?

Sex is good. Intense preoccupation with it is not. Between 3 and 6 percent of Americans—primarily men—spend an inordinate amount of time thinking about sex or acting on their thoughts, neglecting their jobs, relationships, and other aspects of day-to-day life.

14

Fears and Secrets

✗ THINK YOU'RE GOOD IN BED?

Most people believe they could use some help with their bedroom technique. Only 35 percent consider themselves skilled lovers with Italians least confident (only 23 percent regard themselves as masters in bed), followed by the English (28 percent). A third of both Americans and Mexicans (32 percent) see themselves as sexually adept, and despite the reputation Frenchmen have—or perhaps because they're intimidated by living up to it—just 34 percent of them deem themselves above average. On the other hand, 45 percent of Dutch, 46 percent of Chinese, and 49 percent of Spaniards consider themselves sexual pros.

✗ WORRIED YOU'RE NOT GOOD IN BED?

Two out of every five guys worry about being able to perform. At the same time, 42 percent of men and 23.5 percent of women fear they're not pleasuring their partner adequately.

EVER BEEN TOLD YOU WEREN'T SO HOT IN BED?

What a shattering condemnation! Happily, most people have never heard it. But more than 9 percent of both men and women say that they have been sorely wounded by this painful charge, even though in most cases it was justified.

DO YOU FEAR REJECTION WHEN ASKING FOR TENDERNESS?

Men want affection: 38 percent wish they could ask their spouse for more of it but they fret that looking for more cuddling brands them a sissy. Thirty percent wish they could talk openly with their wife about spiritual matters and 26 percent of men and women wish their partners would ask them questions about themselves.

ARE YOU WORRIED ABOUT AIDS?

Maybe you're not, but 27 percent of people worldwide would have sex more often if they weren't concerned about contracting the virus. Four in ten Americans say AIDS is the biggest boogeyman dampening their sexual appetite. One in five of both sexes also worry a lot about other sexually transmitted diseases.

EVER BEEN TESTED FOR AIDS?

This very much depends on who you are. According to the National Center for Health Statistics, just 15 percent of sexually active adults have taken the test. Other surveys show almost three times that. Not surprisingly, more men have been tested than women, but the gap is narrowing.

ARE YOU SPOOKED ABOUT CONTRACTING ANOTHER STD?

AIDS is the big threat. Compared to that, just 4 percent are actively concerned about other sexually transmitted diseases. Fewer than one in ten of us has been tested for syphilis or gonorrhea. Yet each year 12 million new people get infected with one and one in five is now walking around with a viral STD.

WOULD YOU TELL YOUR PARTNER IF YOU HAD HERPES?

If they'd had any sexually transmitted infection, seven in ten people claim they would tell their partners.

DO YOU FRET ABOUT GETTING PREGNANT EVERY TIME YOU HAVE SEX?

This is perfectly normal. Twenty-three percent of women fret that they'll get pregnant, and 15.2 percent of men fear they'll be the reason. But 40 percent of women *don't* actively worry about it. Neither do 56 percent of guys.

HAVE YOU EVER FEARED A DATE?

One in five women say that they have been frightened, not so much of intentional harm, but of a violent temper tantrum or other erratic behavior that could get them into an accident.

DO YOU WORRY ABOUT YOUR BIOLOGICAL CLOCK?

Who wouldn't, with all the reminders that time is passing? Thirty-seven percent of women fear, with varying degrees of acuteness, that they won't get married in time to have kids or that they won't conceive before their eggs deplete.

ARE YOU WORRIED ABOUT THE SIZE OF YOUR VAGINA OR PENIS? DERRIERE?

Few men have ever said so directly, but 41 percent of women fret that they're not tight enough to satisfy their partners. For 11 percent of women the hint has not been so subtle. Forty-six percent of guys admit that to a greater or lesser degree the thought that they're not big enough to please women has plagued them. One in five feels crestfallen and nervous about how he hangs. Seventeen percent of folks imagine that their butt is the butt of jokes.

WHAT DISTURBS YOU MOST WHEN YOU'RE NUDE IN FRONT OF YOUR PARTNER?

For women it's weight: 46 percent fret that they're too fat. For men it's their shape—that they're out of it (27 percent), although one in five is anxious about the size of his penis. Forty-four percent of those who don't exercise regularly and 30 percent who do, have felt too fat to f——. So have two-thirds of those eating high-fat diets *and* a third of healthy eaters.

OTHER THAN OVERALL WEIGHT, WHAT'S THE BODY PART CAUSING STRESS?

Get it off your chest; worrying about this is par for the course. Just 18 percent of women are at ease with their breasts. Twelve percent feel self-conscious about their gams and 46 percent worry about the rolls on their belly.

GUYS, EVER WONDER IF THE BABY IS REALLY YOURS?

Check out the eyes, the chin, the cheek formation. More than six out of ten men acknowledge that they have had the occasional doubt about their child's parentage.

HAVE YOU EVER KEPT SECRETS FROM YOUR SPOUSE?

Half of us claim to tell our spouses *everything*. But an equal number believe that not only is it not necessary, but it's often detrimental, and that lies are the glue that keep them together. Indeed, 42 percent of men and 36 percent of women admit keeping something from their mates. Boomers, big-wage earners, and those married a long time are the most likely to have secrets.

WHAT ISSUE IS MOST FREQUENTLY HUSHED-UP?

If you're hiding a price tag so your spouse won't see what you spent, you've got company. Almost half of husbands and wives (48 percent) admit they don't always tell the truth about how much they paid for something. A close runner-up is covering up for the kids—concealing something about Junior's behavior or grades. Eighteen percent of wives confess they've kept mum about the kids and 20 percent of men have concealed a failure at work from their wives. And 6 percent of men and 3 percent of women have kept an eating disorder secret. Eight percent of men have furtively checked out porn online.

DOES YOUR SPOUSE KNOW ABOUT YOUR PRIOR LOVE LIFE?

Maybe it's because curiosity killed the cat but only 62 percent of women and 52 percent of men say their spouses know everything about their past loves. Another 38 percent say their partners only knows some things, either because the mate has not asked for more information (22 percent), or because he or she is only prepared to share a certain amount (17 percent). Only one in ten men and one in twenty women won't share their past with their current partners.

WHAT ABOUT A CURRENT ATTRACTION?
Nineteen percent of men and 10 percent of women have kept secret the fact that they felt attracted to another person. Thirty-eight percent of Americans believe they've had a secret admirer at some point in their lives. Two out of five of us (39 percent) have secretly sent an anonymous love note to a crush. And 48 percent have received a letter or gift from a secret admirer.

DO YOU KEEP YOUR HOPES AND DREAMS TO YOURSELF?
It may not be an impossible dream that one in five people cherish, but it's certainly a hush-hush one. Fifty-six percent of those who won't disclose it to their spouse are just longing to travel together more. For 53 percent the dream involves relocating, and for 41 percent, starting over in a new career. Ten percent keep mum about longing for a dog. At the opposite end of the spectrum two out of three tell their partner about their sexual fantasies.

DO YOU SECRETLY WISH YOU COULD LIVE ON YOUR OWN FOR A WHILE?
Twenty-one percent have, at one time or another, secretly longed to live on their own for a spell.

DO YOU STILL PINE FOR THAT SOMEONE OF OLD?
Nearly one in every three of us (30 percent) recall one past relationship that we wish would have continued. That includes 19 percent of those happily married to someone else.

15

Firsts and Young Love

WHEN DID YOU LOSE YOUR VIRGINITY . . . OR, AS SOME SAY, FIND YOUR CENTER?

Maybe it's the steamy movies and sitcoms or perhaps peer pressure, but more than half of all Americans have crossed that great divide by the time they're eighteen. The global average for first-time sex is 15.9 years. By age fifteen, according to the National Center for Health Statistics, a third of girls have done it (versus less than 5 percent in 1970), as have 45 percent of boys (up from 20 percent in 1972). In the U.S., northeasterners and midwesterners are the laggards: 58 percent of them have had sex by age eighteen, whereas 65 percent of westerners have done it by then as have 82 percent of southerners. Priests may grimace but 60 percent of Catholic girls say they've "sinned" by eighteen as have 76 percent of Catholic boys. Only 14 percent were still virgins by age twenty-one.

HOW OLD WAS YOUR PARTNER WHEN YOU LOST YOUR VIRGINITY?

More than half (51 percent) say their first-time experience was with someone under seventeen. For 27 percent of people their introduction was with someone eighteen to twenty, and for 21 percent it was with an adult.

WAS YOUR FIRST WITH A SERIOUS BOYFRIEND OR GIRLFRIEND?

For one in three of us the encounter was more of a casual one-night stand than part of an enduring and devoted relationship. Sadly, for 2 percent, their first sexual experience was the result of rape or incest.

WHO KNOWS WHEN AND WHERE THE FIRST TIME MAY BE?

Spring may be associated with love but it's summer when most adolescents experience this rite of passage. Almost half of teens (46 percent) had their first sexual experience between May and August. Summer remains peak season for newbie twenty-somethings, but not by as great a margin. More than a third (35 percent) stole back to their parents' house to do the deed, while 14 percent staked out the backseat. Seven percent took to the bushes.

DO YOU REMEMBER WHAT YOU WERE THINKING THAT FIRST TIME?

Hard to recall, but for those who do, their main concerns were about how they were performing, and the dire consequences if they didn't use protection. (Some 26 percent of people did not.) It certainly wasn't universally wonderful: 37 percent were disappointed. Only 19 percent remember it as a better experience than they'd expected.

WHAT WAS THE MAIN INCENTIVE FOR YOUR FIRST SEXUAL RELATIONSHIP?

Chalk it up to curiosity for the guys; it was the prime motivation for 37 percent of them. Another 29 percent were in love and doing what comes naturally, while 11 percent simply seized the opportunity. Six percent, feeling pressure, obliged their partner and 5 percent just wanted to get it over with.

AT WHAT AGE DID YOU LEARN THE CORRECT NAMES FOR CERTAIN BODY PARTS?

By the time we're two, most of us know rudimentary anatomy. The slang terms come a bit later, like fourth grade. By three or four, most kids are touching themselves, playing doctor with neighborhood kids, and asking Mom and Dad how they got here. By the time they're thirteen or fourteen, eight out of ten have had a boyfriend or girlfriend—and half of those are going out on dates.

AT WHAT AGE DID YOU FIRST KISS SOMEONE ROMANTICALLY?

We're not talking about a peck on the cheek. Seventy-nine percent of young teens have really kissed, in a deep and romantic way. The first kiss is often the most memorable: 33 percent of men and women say they never got over the person with whom they shared it.

HOW ABOUT PETTING?

They used to call it second base: nowadays it's like the entrance gate. By age fourteen, more than half of all boys have fondled a girl's breasts, and one in four has fingered a girl. By age eighteen, more than three out of four have engaged in heavy petting. Fifty-five percent of teens say they've experienced fellatio or cunnilingus.

DID YOU DO IT ON PROM NIGHT?

Forget the corsage—bring the Kama Sutra. Almost half of all teens (45 percent) expect to go all the way prom night. More than one in four (28 percent) anticipate doing it at a rented hotel room, 23 percent aim to cozy up in the back of the car, and 4 percent to go to a friend's house.

DID YOU QUESTION YOUR SEXUAL ORIENTATION AS AN ADOLESCENT?

Most gays claim to have known they were different in their early double digits. Uncertainty about sexual orientation is common among preteens. Twenty-six percent of twelve-year-olds admit they're unsure about their leanings. But that diminishes with age; only 5 percent of eighteen-year-olds wonder if they're straight.

DID YOU MARRY THE FIRST PERSON YOU GOT TO KNOW IN A BIBLICAL SENSE?

Seventeen percent of us had our first sexual experience with the person we ultimately married. Two out of five who've been married have hooked up with their first love. And hold on to your hats for this: 29 percent of Americans were virgins when they married, with virgin marriages highest in the region that includes New York and Washington D.C. (36 percent).

IF YOUR FIRST LOVE WAS SO GREAT, WHY THE SPLIT?

One in four (24 percent) blamed geography; one or the other of the lovers moved away. Twelve percent of relationships expired for lack of interest. For 9 percent the split was caused by another person and 6 percent attribute the breakup to a classic lovers' quarrel.

DID YOU TALK TO YOUR KIDS ABOUT THE BIRDS AND THE BEES?

We'd rather talk to our kids about sex than about money, but still we'd rather watch *The West Wing* than talk about either. Two out of three parents feel awkward discussing sex with their children, about the same percent who say *their* parents didn't talk to them about it. But somewhere between 44 and 55 percent squelch their awkwardness to do it anyway.

SO HOW DID YOU FIRST LEARN ABOUT SEX?

Chances are it wasn't from Mom and Dad. Only one in five consider their parents their primary news source. Rather they learned from friends (29 percent). Sex education in school was the main channel for 16 percent and the first sexual encounter—the school of the world, so to speak—was prime training ground for 9 percent. Five percent heard about it from siblings or other relatives and four percent read the scoop in magazines or books or watched it on the screen.

DO YOU STILL HOLD A CANDLE FOR YOUR FIRST LOVE?

No matter how many years have passed or romantic experiences they've had, one in four people remember their first love with fondness and longing. These torchbearers tend to be single. Thirty-four percent are eighteen to thirty-four years old and 31 percent forty-five to fifty-four. We accept the fact that we're essentially revisionists: eighty-one percent of people concede that the memory of their first time is better than the reality of it.

HAVE YOU EVER TRIED TO FIND YOUR FIRST LOVE?

One in five people has gone looking. Of those who've succeeded, 41 percent were happy to be just friends, yet 19 percent (mostly men) were still spellbound. Nine percent of all women were disappointed in what they found.

16

Love Is in the Air

Three out of four people in America profess to be in love right now. More than four out of five who aren't, are out there looking for it. If it doesn't make the world go 'round, at least it keeps us spinning.

HOW ROMANTIC ARE YOU?

The Earth may be experiencing global warming, but Americans' romantic register is not exactly soaring. A recent Society of American Florists survey suggests our collective romantic climate registers fizzle, not sizzle. Fewer than one in five (19 percent) men ranked themselves as a seven or higher on a romantic scale of one to ten. Apparently, they see themselves accurately—or at least as the object of their affection (or lack of it) sees them. Nineteen percent of women rate their boyfriend, husband, or significant other as at least a seven. The remaining 81 percent of men rank their romantic temperature as anywhere from mild to downright chilly.

DO YOU BELIEVE IN LOVE AT FIRST SIGHT?

Seeing each other across a crowded room and knowing that he or she is the one is a bunk Hollywood fantasy says one in four of us. But two out of three believe in Cupid's arrow. Three-fifths of those married for two years or less claim they fell in love at first sight. Twice as many men as women say it happened to them: 86 percent vs. 41 percent of women.

WHAT WOULD BE A TRULY ROMANTIC EVENING?

Anything without the kids, say 11 percent of parents. Fifty-eight percent consider an evening of movies and Beaujolais before the fireplace to be close to heaven. For 31 percent romance plays out as a night out at a favorite restaurant. Twenty-two percent say they go out of their way to be romantic all the time; 8 percent wonder how they have the time or inclination.

HOW OFTEN DO YOU UTTER THOSE THREE LITTLE WORDS?

I love you, I love you, I love you. You can't say it too much, although 35 percent of people surely try. They say it constantly! On the other hand, 44 percent who actually have someone in their lives whom they love concede that they probably don't say it enough. Similarly, 35 percent wouldn't think to leave a love note on the pillow or a poem on the fridge. They abandoned the game when their partner did and it's no fun playing alone. But in 41 percent of couples at least one of the partners often surprises the other with a feel-good phone call. Twenty-four percent leave love notes for their sweetie as a matter of course.

DO YOU SLEEP LIKE SPOONS?

Almost 70 percent of those who share a bed start off spooning—that is, nestled together—and then, as they settle in and drift off to sleep, they separate to sleep on their sides.

HAVE YOU EVER SIPPED CHAMPAGNE FROM A SLIPPER?

Love prompts those under its spell to do some pretty weird things. Almost one in ten (9.4 percent) of daring and romantic souls out there admit that they've sipped champagne from a shoe or slipper—or would do so.

WHAT'S THE BEST WAY TO PUT SOME SIZZLE IN YOUR SITUATION?

A good heart-to-heart talk almost always does the trick for 47 percent of pairs, while a vacation without the kids injects instant pizzazz into 26 percent of tepid relationships. For 24 percent a night out for two is good to go. Three percent rely on romantic gifts to reinvigorate the heat.

HAVE YOU THOUGHT ABOUT RENEWING YOUR MARRIAGE VOWS?

The trend is growing. In some areas of the country, such as Sacramento, wedding vow renewals account for 30 percent of ceremonies according to the Association for Wedding Professionals International. Some proclaim they "still do" to celebrate passage through a bad patch; others to show their kids how important their bond is.

DO YOU USUALLY END PHONE CALLS TO YOUR HONEY WITH AN "I LOVE YOU"?

Our passion may not be engaged, but our vocal cords certainly are. Four out of ten of us sign off personal phone calls with that magical code. In all but business letters, "love" has replaced "sincerely" as the de rigueur ending, making it more ubiquitous than the happy face in its day. And some 45 percent of us tell our significant other how much we love them more than once a day.

WHO SAID "I LOVE YOU" FIRST?

Usually it's the guy who takes the initiative: only 37 percent of the time it was the woman who uttered it first.

DO YOU SAY "I LOVE YOU" WHEN YOU MEET AND PART OR DURING SEX?

Sixty percent of couples utter it when they come together and break away and 55 percent regularly punctuate their sexual encounters with these declarations. Thirty-seven percent just blurt it out randomly, whenever Cupid's arrow prompts them.

WHICH IS MORE EXCITING: FALLING IN LOVE OR GREAT SEX?

That depends on where you call home. While 81 percent of North Americans consider falling in love to be more exciting than great sex (9 percent), only 69 percent of Europeans agree. And yes, you can have great sex without love: 67 percent of Europeans and 56 percent of North Americans concur.

IS IT POSSIBLE TO BE IN LOVE WITH TWO PEOPLE AT THE SAME TIME?

Seems our European cousins are more skilled at juggling. Sixty percent of Europeans say you can love two people at the same time— certainly the Mormons do—but only 44 percent of North Americans agree.

WHAT'S THE MOST ROMANTIC MOVIE YOU EVER SAW?

A recent survey by Blockbuster found the all-time most romantic movie moments are from *Doctor Zhivago* (1965), *Out of Africa* (1985), and *Ghost* (1990). The video chain found a third of all moviegoers consider the scene in *Doctor Zhivago* when Omar Sharif writes Julie Christie a poem at the frozen country estate to represent the epitome of romance. The scene in *Out of Africa* where Robert Redford washes Meryl Streep's hair by the river came in second (25 percent), followed by the scene in *Ghost* when Patrick Swayze and Demi Moore are modeling clay (21 percent). Twelve percent voted for Cary Grant walking into Deborah Kerr's bedroom and seeing the painting she bought that he'd painted in *An Affair to Remember* and 9 percent picked the final scene in *Casablanca* when Humphrey Bogart tells Ingrid Bergman she has to get on the plane. "I'm no good at being noble, but it doesn't take much to see that the problems of three little people don't amount to a hill of beans in this crazy world. Someday you'll understand that. Now, now . . . Here's looking at you, kid."

17

Objets d'Amour

Mary Kay Cosmetics founder Mary Kay Ash used to say that there were two things people want more than sex and money: recognition and praise. Research suggests there are a lot of other things they can't live without—or at least, don't want to.

ON A CHILLY WINTER'S NIGHT, WHAT WOULD YOU MOST LIKE TO CUDDLE WITH?

A significant other wins (50 percent) but not by the expected landslide. Eighteen percent opted to snuggle up with a paperback book and 19 percent prefer to nuzzle their pets. Six percent would rather get cozy with a pint of creamy ice cream and 4 percent with their Palm Pilots.

COULD YOU FORGO SEX OR CIGS?

Nearly 80 percent of smokers say they would rather go without sex for a month than live without their cigarettes. Although three out of five say they would try to quit if their addiction affected their love life, 35 percent admitted they have never attempted to stop smoking.

'FESS UP, IS YOUR REMOTE CONTROL YOUR BEST FRIEND?

It is for 8 percent of us. Two percent describe it as their worst enemy. Most (29 percent) consider the TV remote a power tool, while 18 percent regard it as an extension of themselves. Four percent regard it as a security blanket, and 1 percent as the other man or woman. The rest don't even think about it. A survey from Magnavox found twice as many women as men would rather give up sex than their domination of the TV remote control for one week.

HOW ABOUT YOUR COMPUTER?

Forty-four percent of those who use the Internet say it's become as essential as air in their lungs. If stranded on a desert island, 67 percent say they'd rather have Net access than TV or phone service. Microsoft found that one in four Brits would rather play with their computers than have sex and one in five Swedes enjoy privately stroking their machines.

LADIES, IF YOU HAD TO FORFEIT ONE ITEM OF MAKEUP, WHICH WOULD YOU RELINQUISH?

Not the mascara or blush. Eighty-two percent of women say they wouldn't part with those treasures for all the orange juice in Florida. Three out of four would fight to keep their lipstick.

WHICH FOOD WOULD BE THE LAST YOU FORFEITED?

Call them French fries or freedom fries, no matter, because hands down they are the food more people order at a restaurant than any other. If money's no object, more of us would order steak as an entrée than anything else, despite the bad rap it gets.

DID YOU HAVE A SECURITY BLANKET OR ATTACHMENT OBJECT GROWING UP?

More than six of every ten American kids have treasured a stuffed animal or cuddly blanket like Linus carried around. One in five grown women—and one in twenty adult men—acknowledge that they regularly sleep with a stuffed animal.

DO YOU HAVE A SHOE FETISH?

Thirty-six percent of people concede that they are hooked on footwear, either inexplicably obsessed or devoted to it. It seems to be a female bias.

HOW ABOUT ICE CREAM?

Whether eating it in bed, keeping a secret stash in the freezer, or having a bowl for breakfast, 70 percent of us admit to having at least one ice cream indiscretion. Twenty-six percent have eaten ice cream instead of a meal and 19 percent have taken it to bed. Twenty-two percent find it erotic and have shared a single container with two spoons and a loved one.

DO YOU REALLY LOVE YOUR CAR?

Given the choice between spending a Saturday afternoon with their significant other or polishing the car, more people opt to share the day with their mates. But put pedal to the metal, and cars quickly accelerate our amour-meters. More than three out of four of us (78 percent) say they really love their cars. And 43 percent consider the four-wheeled object in the garage as a real-life member of the family.

DO YOU HAVE A PET NAME FOR YOUR CAR . . . AND DO YOU TALK TO IT?

Two-thirds (67 percent) call their cars by pet names and 63 percent carry on conversations with their cars. Fifty-seven percent consider an old car "a beloved member of the family," while just 43 percent see it as a junky clunker. Twelve percent have even christened the car for good luck.

WHERE IN THE FAMILY LINEUP DOES BESSIE COME?

More than one in four (27 percent) love their car more than their mothers-in-law. But in-laws aren't alone in getting a cold shoulder: 10 percent of married people consider their cars more important than their spouses and 6 percent rated them as more crucial than their kids.

DO YOU KEEP YOUR CAR'S PICTURE ON YOUR DESK OR IN YOUR WALLET?

Fifty-three percent of us carry around a photo of our car or keep it on the desk at work for others to admire.

DO YOU MIND WHEN SOMEONE ELSE TAKES YOUR CAR FOR A SPIN?

"Mind" would be an understatement: 71 percent say they are so protective of their cars that they'd *really* rather no one else drives them and even avoid valet parking.

DO YOU USUALLY BUY YOUR CAR HOLIDAY GIFTS?

For most of us that's going too far down the road, but 12 percent usually treat their wheels to a Valentine's Day gift. And if they could afford only one item, they are almost three times more likely to buy a new car stereo (42 percent) and over two times more likely to have their car detailed (34 percent) than they are to buy expensive perfume or cologne for their sweetie pie (15 percent). Truck owners, it seems are the most devoted: 22 percent celebrate Valentine's Day with their vehicle compared to 9 percent of those who own luxury or full-size vehicles and 6 percent of SUV owners.

DO YOU JUDGE SOMEONE BY THE CAR THEY DRIVE?

Thirty percent of us admit that we judge dates by the type of car they drive. Sure it's superficial but one in four of us admit that we've borrowed someone else's car to impress a date. And 86 percent have washed or prepared their vehicle in some way before picking up a date. Thirty-seven percent would like to see a sports car pull up in the driveway, while 27 percent hope it's a luxury car, and 17 percent, a limo.

DO YOU THINK OF YOUR CAR AS A ROLLING SINGLES CLUB?

Sixty-two percent of folks have used their car as a flirtation station, flirting with other drivers and pedestrians while on the go. Thirty-one percent say at least once it has resulted in a date. Twenty-six percent have followed another car in hopes of securing a date.

WHAT DO YOU MOST LIKE TO DO IN THE CAR?

It's not what you think. Twenty percent say that talking is their favorite car date activity—more than anything else.

DO YOU REMEMBER YOUR MANNERS IN THE CAR?

Seventy-seven percent of guys claim they open and close doors for their dates but only 25 percent expect this when they are a passenger.

HAVE YOU EVER USED EXCUSES TO GET A DATE ALONE IN THE CAR?

"Ever?" Duh, of course. The most popular excuses: getting lost (used by 21 percent), followed by engine trouble, running out of gas, flat tire, and dead battery.

HAVE YOU EVER BEEN PROPOSED TO IN THE CAR?

Fourteen percent have received or made marriage proposals in an automobile.

18

Puppy Love

Humans have their charms, but they can't measure up to pets on the love-o-meter. As a society we're doggone nuts over our animal companions. They're members of 55 million American families. We own—or are owned by—66 million cats, 58 million dogs, 88 million fish, 40 million birds, 13 million small animals (including rabbits, hamsters, and gerbils), and 8 million reptiles. And we shell out more than $24 billion a year on these critters. If that's not love, what is?

DOES PRINCE HAVE YOU WRAPPED AROUND HIS PAWS?
Ninety-five percent of us hug and play with our pets daily. Thirty-five percent take them shopping and 19 percent have brought them to work. And, according to Ralston Purina, 16 percent have taken their dog to a restaurant or bar. Forty-five percent of pet owners won't leave home without them; they've taken the cuddlers on vacation.

DO YOU WHISPER WORDS OF ENDEARMENT TO YOUR FURRY FRIEND?

Most pet owners don't need a holiday to tell their buddies how much they adore them. Sixty-three percent murmur "I wuv you" to their pet at least once a day. Seventy-eight percent of pet owners regularly talk to their pet in a different voice. A third call him or her from the road or office.

DO YOU CARRY AROUND YOUR PET'S PHOTO?

Fifty-three percent of human companions carry a picture of their pets in their wallets. Forty-three percent display their photos at work.

HOW MUCH TIME EACH DAY DO YOU SPEND WITH YOUR PET?

One in five people claim they spend four to eight hours a day romping with Rover. Another 22 percent estimate that they spend even more time together.

DOES DUKE GO TO THE DOC MORE THAN YOU DO?

More pet owners bring their pets to the vet than take themselves to their own doctors for physicals. Two-thirds of pets get shots and checkups more often their than human custodians, according to the American Animal Hospital Association. More than nine out of ten pet owners take their charges for regular veterinary checkups and vaccinations and 82 percent have had their pets spayed or neutered. Sixty-one percent have shelled out more than a thousand dollars on one vet visit. Fewer than 5 percent of pet owners have pet insurance.

DO YOU THINK OF YOURSELF AS DUCHESS'S PARENT?

Eighty-four percent of "human companions" refer to themselves as their pets' "mom" or "dad." And 72 percent of married pet owners greet their pet before their mate when they walk in the door.

DO YOU CELEBRATE YOUR PET'S BIRTHDAY?

Blow out the candles. Sixty-three percent of pet owners celebrate their loved ones' birthdays, and 43 percent routinely give their pets a wrapped gift on the occasion.

WHO'S BETTER COMPANY, YOUR HUBBY OR THE DOG?

More than 40 percent of cat and dog owners say they find their pets better company than their partners. Women are most likely to opt to spend time with their pets, with 45 percent saying they prefer being with them, compared with 30 percent of men, according to insurance group Direct Line. Nearly nine out of ten pet owners also say that when they have had a bad day, spending time with their pet makes them feel less stressed. Nearly one in four pet owners gets the lion's share of affection from their animal. Forty-two percent of women and 25 percent of men say their pets are better attuned to their moods than other family members.

DOES CHLOE GET SPECIAL FOODS AS A TESTAMENT OF YOUR LOVE?

The economy may be on the ropes but the premium food biz is booming. More than three out of four of us (76 percent) buy premium pet foods and 52 percent claim they go out of their way to prepare special meals for their animals. Ninety-seven percent concede they occasionally spoil Rover or Fluffy with an excess of love and affection manifested by pet treats or prime cuts.

DO YOU FEED THE LITTLE DARLING AT THE DINNER TABLE?

Forty-four percent of us say even if Lassie doesn't have an assigned seat, she's a welcome guest at the table . . . or at the very least under it. Two out of three pet owners (67.5 percent) say they have or would share an ice cream cone, lick for lick, with their pooch.

DO YOU USUALLY BUY BUZBY VALENTINE'S AND CHRISTMAS GIFTS?

Move over sweetie. More than 17 percent of pets are likely to get more expensive gifts on Valentine's Day than their master gets for his or her human companion, according to Lavalife dating service. Eighty-seven percent include their pet in December holiday celebrations and 62 percent sign their pets' names to holiday cards, according to Hallmark. One in three include pictures of Princess in holiday greetings, and more than six in ten include news of their pets in holiday updates.

HAVE YOU EVER DRESSED YOUR PET IN HUMAN CLOTHING OR A COSTUME?

So that's where your favorite boa went. More than three out of five pet owners share their sweaters and hats and in other ways see their animal companions as human.

HOW ELSE DO YOU CATER TO ROVER AND FLUFFY?

Two out of three animal owners sing or dance for their pets and 53 percent have taken time off from work to care for a sick puppy. That same percent have turned on music specifically to please their pet.

DO YOU LET YOUR PETS SLEEP IN THE BED WITH YOU?

Forget the doggy bed. One in four dogs in this country and 42 percent of cats dream on in the comfort of the big bed.

DOES ROVER WATCH?

If only Fido could speak: what an X-rated movie director he could be. Of the half of us with animals at home—not counting our sex partners—almost half (45.4 percent) allow our pets in the room during sex. Repressed midwesterners are least likely to allow Cleo in as an observer.

WOULD YOU DATE SOMEONE WHO DIDN'T LIKE YOUR PET?

No way, José. Nine out of ten women would drop a potential partner who didn't get along with their pet. Twenty-two percent would refuse to marry a man who didn't like their other beloved. And 40 percent of marriages for pet owners are contingent on the partners' agreeing to keep the beloved. Just 28 percent of masters and mistresses think that if they were issued an ultimatum, they'd part with their pet.

WHAT IF SOMEONE IN YOUR FAMILY DEVELOPED AN ALLERGY TO TRIXIE?

To paraphrase Rodney King, can't we all just live together? Nearly 45 percent of households with allergy sufferers have kept their dog or cat knowing the creature could cause a sickly reaction. Only 23 percent of those have confined the pet to a single area of the house to minimize damage.

WHEN YOUR POOCH PASSES, WOULD YOU PURCHASE A CASKET?

Balmoral in Connecticut used to be the only pet cemetery. Now there are several around the country. Most home-owners bury their dearly departed on their property. Nearly 5 percent have bought a coffin for their pet. Many more made one themselves.

IF CHLOE WERE CATNAPPED, WOULD YOU MORTGAGE THE HOUSE?

If Fifi were held up for ransom, almost one in five pet owners swear they'd pay whatever it took to get him or her back. A recent Gallup poll found that the majority of American pet owners would not be willing to trade their dog or cat for $1 million. On the other hand, an equal number would not pay any ransom.

DO YOU THINK YOU'D RISK YOUR OWN LIFE TO RESCUE YOUR PET?

There are even stories of people risking their own lives to rescue somebody else's pet. Eighty-three percent of pet owners say that while they'd choose their children over their animal, they'd probably put their lives in jeopardy to save that of their pet.

19

Money Matters

WHICH DO YOU THINK ABOUT MORE: COLD CASH OR HOT SEX?
Almost half of people (47 percent) think more about the almighty dollar than their almighty lover, while 17 percent say they think more about sex. For the rest, it's a dead heat. Men (big surprise here) are likelier than women to think more about sex—or at least to claim they do.

OKAY, SO WHICH DO YOU ENJOY MORE: MONEY OR SEX?
Just 35 percent say that hands down, they enjoy sex more than they enjoy money.

WHICH DO YOU WANT MORE: MONEY OR LOVE?
Ninety-two percent of people say they would rather be phenomenally rich than find the love of their lives. More than a third of eighteen- to sixty-four-year-old women consider having enough money more important to the success of a marriage than good sex.

WHAT DO YOU ARGUE ABOUT MORE: SEX OR MONEY?

Money is the number one cause of disagreements in marriages, sparking nearly twice as many rows as sex. Twenty-nine percent of couples say they frequently disagree about whether to spend or save, beating out what to watch on TV as fight fodder. Seventeen percent have ended a relationship because of money.

WHICH DO YOU MANAGE BETTER: LOVE OR MONEY?

More than half (55 percent) acknowledge needing to do a better job managing their financial situations. They think they're on even keel with their romantic affairs.

WOULD YOU SELL YOUR SPOUSE FOR A MILLION DOLLARS?

Two out of three of us, holding tight to those holy vows, wouldn't lend their spouse for a night, even for a million bucks. One in ten would accept this indecent proposal, while 16 percent admit they'd mull it over. Another 13 percent aren't talking.

DO YOU THINK YOUR PARTNER WOULD SIGN A PRENUP IF YOU HAD MORE ASSETS?

Forty-four percent of women trust that their intended would step up and do the right thing but a fourth think Romeo would get writing paralysis. Thirty percent couldn't guess if their mate would affix his John Hancock to a prenuptial.

DO YOU THINK A WOMAN EARNING MORE THAN HER FELLA SPELLS TROUBLE?

It's happening in around one in every four families but 53 percent of women and 34 percent of men feel that the lady bringing home more bacon than her man will lead to dissension in the relationship.

HAVE YOU EVER DATED SOMEONE BECAUSE OF HIS OR HER BANKBOOK?

Just 12 percent of people admit they've given someone a second look or a second chance because of the zeroes on his tax return.

IS IT OKAY TO MARRY FOR MONEY?

What's love got to do with it? According to a Prudential survey, 12 percent of women and 16 percent of men think that it is okay to marry for money. At the same time, a third of women and 26 percent of men think it's very unwise to marry someone who'd be a financial albatross.

DOES THE VALUE OF AN ENGAGEMENT RING MATTER?

Struck by the romanticism of the moment, 78 percent say no. But the rest assign certain criteria to express the importance of what it represents.

WOULD YOU KISS A STRANGER FOR TWO HUNDRED DOLLARS?

A third of us might even smooch with a frog for that quick cash. Another third (31 percent) would need at least five hundred dollars to overcome that shyness. Thirty-seven percent wouldn't be interested even at that price. Then again, three out of four people say they'd kiss a frog for just fifty dollars.

WOULD YOU RATHER TALK TO YOUR PARENTS ABOUT SEX OR MONEY?

Young adults would rather ask their parents about sex than either discuss their finances with them or ask for a loan. Why, it's even easier to ask Mom and Dad if Carol/Carl can stay overnight in their bedroom than go over their portfolio.

WOULD YOU DRESS MORE REVEALINGLY TO DOUBLE YOUR SALARY?

Just about half of us (47.5 percent) would hike up our skirts and show some cleavage if it meant doubling our pay. The rest consider that an unscrupulous sellout.

WOULD YOU UNDERGO A SEX CHANGE FOR ALL THE MONEY YOU'D EVER NEED?

Even if it were reversible, only 15 percent would consider trading their gender for an endless allowance, according to Dreamscape.

HOW FAR WOULD YOU GO FOR $10 MILLION?
The truth is, most of us would do just about anything. A quarter would abandon all their friends and church or become a prostitute for a week.

WOULD YOU HAVE SEX FOR MONEY?
Sixty percent of us dismiss the idea flat-out, but 6.7 percent think getting paid for something they enjoy doing sounds like a good deal. For another 12.5 percent it depends on how much money and sex is involved and 20.4 percent say it depends on who with.

WOULD YOU POSE NUDE IN A MAGAZINE FOR MONEY?
Not on your life, say half of us. But 11.7 percent say why not? For the rest it depends on the amount of money proffered and their own need for it.

DO YOU TRUST YOUR PARTNER WITH YOUR MONEY?
Forty percent of folks say it's madness to trust anyone else with your money—even your husband, wife, or steady partner. Fourteen percent don't even let their spouses know their pin numbers.

DO YOU KNOW HOW MUCH YOUR SPOUSE MAKES?
What we make is apparently the last taboo. Three out of ten husbands and wives are in the dark. Our collective secretiveness about what we take home extends to other family members. Just 26 percent of moms and 19 percent of dads know how much their kids earn and 19 percent of children know what their parents make. We'd rather talk about a friend's marital problems (55 to 47 percent) than shaky finances.

IS IT OKAY FOR MARRIED FOLKS TO KEEP SEPARATE ACCOUNTS?
Two-thirds of us think it's fine for a husband or wife to have an account outside joint terrain, but one in four thinks it indicates lack of trust. More than one in every three of us (36 percent) have both a separate and joint account. A fourth maintain only a joint account. Twenty-two percent keep separate accounts. (The rest are single.)

DO YOU HAVE A SECRET STASH?

More than 60 percent of people hoard a private pile of cash in a bid to safeguard against the possibility of a breakup. Almost three-quarters of women admitted to having hidden money from their other half, compared to 53 percent of men.

IF YOU BORROW MONEY FROM YOUR MATE, DO YOU PAY IT BACK?

Fewer than one in three of us diligently pay back money we borrow from our partners. Others see it as a gift.

SHOULD HE OR SHE WHO MAKES THE LION'S SHARE OF DOUGH MAKE THE LION'S SHARE OF DECISIONS?

Political correctness wins out. Seven out of ten people insist on joint decision-making. Even so, a fourth aver that money should talk.

WHO DOES THE CHECKBOOK?

In households where money is pooled, three out of five times it's the wives keeping the books: 56 percent take sole responsibility for paying the bills. The family budget on the other hand is still pretty much a guy thing: just 36 percent of women take control here.

DO YOU THINK YOUR SEX LIFE IMPROVED WHEN YOUR FINANCES DID?

There seems to be a correlation here. Fifty-eight percent of people say a bull market is better than a case of Viagra. Twenty-two percent see no difference but at least the bills get paid. The rest wonder, what sex life.

WHO SHOULD PAY FOR THE DATE?

Despite the concept of equality, more than half of us (54 percent) say the guy should almost always underwrite the event. But 31 percent believe they should go dutch and 13 percent believe that if the lass earns more, she should fork over the dough. Others grumble that the thing to do is split it or take turns.

HOW ABOUT WHEN SHE INVITES HIM TO DINNER?

Two-thirds of people (65 percent) say when the woman does the inviting, she should do the underwriting. Thirty percent say even then, the man should at least reach for his wallet.

CAN MONEY BUY LOVE?

Seventy-one percent of us say unequivocally no, but 21 percent think it definitely opens the door. Another 8 percent aren't sure but think a pot of gold is worth a lot more than a poke in the eye.

IF MONEY DOESN'T MATTER, DOES ITS ABSENCE?

Women may not necessarily want to date the guy with big bucks, but they almost surely will spurn the one with very few of them. More women would rather date a man who is unavailable than one who is broke.

20

On the Job

A decade ago, a government study found that nearly a third of all romances began on the job. Today, with the workforce 46 percent female, and employees putting in longer hours, the number of workplace-inspired romances should be even higher. Four out of five staffers have either participated in a romance or observed a colleague's at their workplace. In a third of these romances one (or both) of the participants is married—to someone else.

HAVE YOU EVER DATED SOMEONE IN THE OFFICE?
It's pretty common. Some 28 percent of workers have gone out with a colleague. Even more have had a secret crush on a coworker: 53 percent of single male office workers and a third of women clandestinely admire a fellow colleague.

DID YOU MEET YOUR SIGNIFICANT OTHER ON THE JOB?
Eliminating the marriages that weren't arranged, approximately 23 percent of current couples got their spark at work—including that of Microsoft multibillionaire founder Bill Gates and Melinda French,

a Microsoft marketing executive, who wed each other in 1993. An American Management Association survey found that fully half the time the result of a workplace romance is either marriage or a long-term connection—better odds than for nonworkplace romances.

DOES YOUR COMPANY HAVE A FORMAL DATING POLICY?

Who knows? A fourth of workers claim to have no idea what their companies' rules are on this front. No wonder; only 13 percent of companies have official antiromance policies, according to the Society for Human Resource Management. In contrast, 43 percent have formal rules about displaying nude pictures or obscene cartoons at work. Amazingly, 86 percent of workers don't know that a man has to be told explicitly that his advances aren't welcome to meet the legal definition of harassment.

WHAT'S RESTRICTED IN THE WORKPLACE?

Among companies with policies, 70 percent ban romance between supervisor and subordinate and 19 percent bar it between two people in the same department and 4 percent, on the same project. Thirteen percent disallow a relationship between employee and customer or client and in 4 percent of companies workers cannot date someone who works for a competitor. Three percent won't let their employees date vendors. Fifteen percent require those romantically connected to inform their supervisors of the relationship and 11 percent articulate that those so involved may not report to the same supervisor. Thirty-seven percent prohibit public displays of affection.

DO YOU THINK OFFICE ROMANCES CRIMP PRODUCTIVITY?

Twice as many people think it hurts more than it helps (16 percent vs. 8 percent). But most feel it doesn't make a difference either way. Research studies suggest they're wrong, that once employees get past the initial infatuation stage of being unable to concentrate on anything but their new love, an office romance raises worker morale, stimulates performance, enhances creativity, and boosts productivity. If it turns into a long-term commitment, companies can gain happier, loyal employees.

DO YOU THINK A WORKPLACE DALLIANCE INCREASES FAVORITISM?

There's the rub: 86 percent think it's a slippery slope. Seventy-eight percent say that even if they don't increase favoritism, they can create an unbusinesslike appearance and 77 percent feel they expose the company to the danger of sexual harassment suits.

DO YOU THINK A COMPANY SHOULD CARE ONE WAY OR ANOTHER ABOUT OFFICE ROMANCES?

Four out of five people (79 percent) think that if an unmarried couple is discreet, their workplace romance should not be anyone's business but their own. But because it has the potential to affect productivity, morale, and even sexual harassment suits, 19 percent think it's fair game as a workplace concern and believe dating a coworker should be against company policy.

DO YOU THINK OFFICE AFFAIRS ARE INEVITABLE?

Given the number of hours people are putting in at their jobs, 51 percent of us expect the number of relationships that percolate here to increase and for office romances to be even more common.

ARE YOU LOOKING FOR LOVE WHILE AT WORK?

Driven by romantic allure, novelty, curiosity, and heavy media promotion, in one recent month eight million at-work Internet users sought romance between the spreadsheets by visiting personals websites. The average workplace visitor to online personals spent fifty-one minutes on the cyberprowl at work versus thirty-seven minutes spent by those clicking in from home.

EVER HAD A BOSS WHO SEXUALLY HARASSED YOU?

Eleven percent of workers claim to have been the victim of a sexually aggressive supervisor. Yet two out ten of the women had sex with their boss and 15 percent of those ended up marrying him. Twenty percent of women and 12 percent of men have slept with an intern.

HAVE YOU EVER TRIED TO CONCEAL AN OFFICE ROMANCE?

It usually doesn't succeed but two out of three couples in a workplace romance try to keep their relationship hush-hush. Most of their coworkers know about it long before they come out of the closet. Only 15 percent intentionally tried to keep their relationship secret because it violated company policy. More compelling reasons for keeping mum include a desire to avoid disruption at work and protecting a spouse, partner, or themselves from that partner's wrath.

HAS YOUR COMPANY HAD A SEXUAL HARASSMENT LAWSUIT RECENTLY?

According to the Society for Human Resource Management, only 4 percent of companies have experienced such lawsuits in the past five years.

HAVE YOU DONE "IT" AT WORK?

Some 44 percent of men and 35 percent of women admit to having had sex on the job. Most of the time it was with their real life partner. But one in five took on this assignment with a coworker during work hours; 23 percent waited until after others had gone home. Thirty-four percent of women and considerably more men have masturbated at work.

WHERE DID YOU DO IT?

The most popular location for workplace sex was an office, preferred by 41 percent. Other places used for sex included the conference room (25 percent), a bathroom stall (23 percent), the office parking lot (21 percent), a cloakroom (16 percent), the elevator (9 percent), the mailroom (9 percent), the cafeteria (7 percent), and in a supply closet (4 percent). Half of folks have used a desk and 48 percent have comingled on a chair. Thirty-seven percent made do with the office floor.

IF YOU COULD, WOULD YOU SLEEP YOUR WAY TO THE TOP?

The old casting-couch routine. One in five women are prepared to sleep with their boss even if they dislike him if it means certain promotion. Forty-one percent of both men and women believe that rumors swirling about people sleeping their way up are true.

DO YOU FLIRT WITH YOUR FELLOW FILERS?

This seems almost universal. Ninety-two percent of workers admit flirting with an attractive coworker—although just 9 percent think the come-ons are serious. Among the 41 percent who follow through, more than half had intercourse. Eight-seven percent kissed, 75 percent petted, and 54 percent, oral sex.

HAS A COWORKER OF THE SAME SEX PURSUED YOU?

One in three has been the object of attention from someone of their own sex but only 2 percent were upset by the overture. Half either flirted back for the fun of it, or actually went out.

WOULD YOU BE FLATTERED IF A COWORKER FLIRTED WITH YOU?

This depends on whether you're a gal or a guy. Forty-seven percent of men would be titillated but only one in four women would be. The rest would be irked.

HAVE YOU EVER GOTTEN CAUGHT WITH YOUR PANTS DOWN OR SKIRT UP AT WORK?

Seven percent of those who've gotten down on the job got caught in the act. Most (87 percent) say the worst repercussion was embarrassment. And 16.3 percent of people say they've interrupted somebody doing it at work.

HAVE YOU EVER MADE SEXUAL REMARKS OR INNUENDOS AT WORK?

Twenty-nine percent of workers say they've intentionally made a double entendre or sly suggestion to a colleague. Thirteen percent have sent a coworker cute or suggestive email, and 41 percent have made prolonged eye contact with a coworker. Thirty-one percent have gone as far as rubbing a colleague's shoulders.

DID YOUR OFFICE ROMANCE LAST LONGER THAN YOUR JOB?

For 17 percent it wasn't even an affair; the fling lasted just a few days or weeks at most. But nearly half of office romances last at least a year and 3 percent culminate in marriage.

HAVE YOU WITNESSED RETALIATION WHEN THE ROMANCE ENDED?

The romance itself may never have interfered with work but its aftermath certainly might. Of those who break off an office duo, 17 percent have seen their rejected beaus take revenge. Twelve percent have been stalked. Five percent of workers have witnessed broken workplace romances lead to physical violence. In 12 percent of relationships, at least one of the members left the company or asked for a transfer after the breakup. And 9 percent said their fling led to separation or divorce for one member of the couple. Three percent were fired for their transgression.

HAVE YOU EVER FANTASIZED ABOUT A COWORKER?

Forty-five percent of workers admit they've imagined how a coworker would look under the sheets. Even more (65 percent) have sensed a coworker mentally undressing them.

DO YOU THINK YOU'VE PAID A PRICE FOR SAYING NO?

It's one of those nebulous areas that's hard to prove but 4 percent of women and 1 percent of men believe they've suffered for rebuffing a supervisor's or manager's advances. Three out of four feel they did not lose their perches on the ladder to someone who was closer than close with their boss. Three times as many women feel a far bigger problem than losing out to the beneficiaries of sexual-conferred favoritism is the "old boys' club."

DO YOU DRESS TO STIR THE EMBERS AT THE OFFICE?

A third of women and a fourth of men think that they play up their sexuality at work—more than the numbers who strive to deemphasize it. Only one in four women feels that strutting their stuff has been a boon for them.

HAVE YOU EVER FEARED ACTING FRIENDLY MAY BE MISCONSTRUED?

Not everyone is jumping to conclusions. Still, 15 percent of women and 9 percent of men are reluctant to befriend a coworker out of fear that he or she might read it as an unwanted advance.

HAVE YOU EVER TAKEN OFF FROM WORK TO MAKE WHOOPIE?

If you haven't, get with the program. Over half of workers under age thirty have phoned in sick so they could do something else in the sack than cough and so have 24 percent of those over fifty. (Impressive, but shy of the 56 percent of folks who've taken time off because they need to nurse a hangover.)

DO YOU CONNECT BETTER WITH COWORKERS THAN WITH YOUR MATE?

Women are not as plagued by this as men but 30 percent of workaholic guys say they find they have more in common with their female colleagues than with their wives.

IS IT OKAY TO LET YOUR HAIR DOWN AT THE COMPANY HOLIDAY PARTY?

Unfasten it, but don't let it fly away. Fifty-seven percent of workers think flirting may be the redemption of office parties. But 18 percent warn that it's a tricky floor and you have to be well behaved and professional to avoid slipping on it. Ninety percent of men and 86 percent of women endorse mistletoe at the office bash and, depending on who they're facing there, would pucker up.

HAVE YOU EVER REGRETTED THE WAY YOU BEHAVED AT A COMPANY PARTY?

Wearing the lampshade on your head was the least of it. Fourteen percent of women and 23 percent of men confess to having morning-after regrets for their overly amorous actions at the company party. Altogether, a third of singles believe they've humiliated themselves at an office get-together.

WHAT'S THE RIGHT GIFT TO GIVE AT WORK?

Keep it impersonal. In the office, 36 percent of those receiving gifts from business associates would most appreciate tickets to a sporting or entertainment event, while 23 percent prefer flowers.

ARE YOU A MORE PRODUCTIVE WORKER DURING SEXUAL DROUGHTS?

Fifty-nine percent think they redirect those bedroom energies into greater productivity at work.

WOULD YOU WELCOME WORKING AT THE SAME PLACE AS YOUR MATE?

Too much time together may not be such a good thing. Forty percent would not want to work at the same place, reasoning that love and work don't mix. A third think it could go well if there was enough separation and neither reported directly to the other. Yet a fourth of people regard this as close to heaven.

DO YOU HAVE SOME FRIENDS AT WORK?

In some cases it's more a friendship fair than a job. It's certainly fertile hunting ground. Fifty-three percent of workers have at least a few friends from the job—more than who found them through clubs and organizations (39 percent) and church groups (38 percent). It doesn't take long to make friends at work: 49 percent were bonded after only a few days.

DO YOU SOCIALIZE WITH YOUR COWORKERS OFF THE JOB?

The workplace may not be one big happy family but for 4 percent of us, colleagues replace families. Three out of four consider their coworkers the greatest perk of the job. Only 18 percent avoid interacting with colleagues when they don't have to.

DO YOU LOVE YOUR JOB?

Twenty-eight percent consider it more a friendship than love affair. Twenty-six percent say it will be a bitter breakup. Twenty-two percent admit it started out as a friendship but it's building. Nineteen percent acknowledge it was love at first sight. But for 3 percent, alas, it was close to a one-night stand; they were dumped soon after the relationship began.

21

On the Road

For most of us, the bedroom is hardly the only place to get frisky, although 35 percent prefer to make love there. Where else in the world is a suitable setting?

WHY DON'T WE DO IT ON THE ROAD?

Having sex in the car seems to be a well-ingrained rite of passage. Eighty-four percent of people have made use of the backseat. One in four workers claims to have had sex in the parking lot after a Christmas party. (More than one in six men has injured himself in this line of duty.) One in five of us has even done it in the back of a taxi.

ARE YOU A MEMBER OF THE MILE-HIGH CLUB?

Terrorism has taken its toll. It's harder than ever to have sex in an airplane lavatory these days: only 13 percent of couples say they've made it in the clouds at least once.

DO YOU FLIRT WITH THE FLIGHT ATTENDANT?

Whether you call them stewardesses or air hostesses, they do more than serve and scold: they attract. Nearly one in every ten passengers has flirted with a flight attendant. Three percent of travelers actually wrangled a date with one while on board.

IS SEX OUT OF THIS WORLD?

Four out of five people (79 percent) would rather try sex in space than do any other activity at zero gravity, according to mobile phone services company Zed.

HAVE YOU DONE IT IN THE SHOWER?

While it's a well-known fact that people give their vocal chords a good workout when soaping up, getting dirty while getting clean is also popular. Twenty-nine percent of hotel guests have showered or bathed with a buddy, according to Westin Hotels. Two out of three couples have experienced a hot tub tryst.

HAVE YOU DONE IT AT SCHOOL . . . OR UNDER THE AUSPICES?

If that's in loco parentis, lots of us have very liberal parents. More than a third of students sixteen and under have had some sexual experience while on a supervised school trip. One in five (21 percent) claim to have had intercourse on an overnight field trip.

HOW ABOUT IN THE GREAT OUTDOORS?

No surprise that young folks routinely enjoy doing what comes naturally au naturel, but it seems that baring it all isn't just for the young. One in five couples over age sixty enjoy doing it outside as well. Sixty-two percent have experienced that gritty, grainy sensation of doing it on the beach.

HAVE YOU EVER HAD SEX IN A PUBLIC PLACE?

The playground, parking lot, restaurant bathroom: these are the most common venues for 83 percent of us who've done it in public. For two-thirds it was a one-time adventure but the rest got hooked on the excitement of possible discovery. That's only happened to one in eight couples. One in twenty has been caught by the authorities although very few have been arrested.

WHOSE IDEA WAS IT TO DO IT OUT IN THE OPEN?

Sometimes it's not actually an idea but an impulse. Fourteen percent say it just happened. But when it was a preconceived notion, 22 percent of the time he thought it up and 17 percent of the time, she did. Most often—in 47 percent of cases—they both hit on the idea together.

DOES TRAVELING FOR BUSINESS MAKE YOU FEEL MORE ROMANTIC?

It does for 23 percent of business travelers. There have to be some perks to being a road warrior, say the 14 percent of men and 4 percent of women who look for a discreet encounter on the side or at least are open to a furtive fling on a business trip.

DO YOU THINK YOU'RE LIKELIER TO HAVE A FLING ON A HOLIDAY ABROAD OR CLOSE TO HOME?

Distance makes the difference. How about *nine* times more likely when on the road far away? Yet only 11 percent own up to hoping for a sex adventure if they go away without their partner.

CONGRATULATIONS, YOU'VE WON A FREE HOTEL STAY. WHO WOULD YOU BRING?

Sorry, kids—romantic vacations handily trump family ones (36 to 27 percent) when a gift trip presents itself. Thirty-one percent of couples have taken a romantic getaway in a recent year, according to Travel Industry Association of America. Forty-six percent of travelers brought along a domestic partner on a business trip in the last year.

WHAT ABOUT THE KIDS?

They've accompanied Mom or Dad or both on 15 percent of business trips in a recent year, according to the National Business Travel Association. Eighty-seven percent of parents claim they love to travel with their children. Kids went along on 72 percent of all vacation trips. Twenty percent of those trips also included a third generation of the family.

22

Forgive or Call It Quits?

Every day in America some 3,200 married couples untie the knot after waiting an average twelve months for divorce proceedings to grind their way to a conclusion. The typical divorce ends a marriage of 7.1 years (up from 6.6 years in 1974). The divorce rate hovers around 44 percent, after soaring to 50 percent in the 1980s. Still, more than a million divorce cases are filed annually in this country. No one believes divorce is good but that doesn't mean you can't have a good divorce.

HAVE YOU EVER HAD YOUR HEART BROKEN?
If you haven't, you're a rare bird. Ninety-five percent of people have suffered the pain and despair of unrequited love before their twenty-fifth birthday.

DO YOU EXPECT YOUR MARRIAGE TO LAST FIVE YEARS?
There's a one in five probability that the parties to a first marriage will separate or divorce within five years. The probability for co-habitants splitting in that time frame is more than double—49

percent. Practice does not make perfect. The probability for second marriages failing is 23 percent after five years and 39 percent after a decade.

WHAT'S AGE GOT TO DO WITH IT?
Nearly half of those who marry under age eighteen wind up divorcing, compared to only one-quarter of those who marry after age twenty-five.

WHAT OTHER FACTORS WEIGH IN?
Forty-six percent of those not affiliated with a religion and 43 percent of women whose parents divorced, also unravel the knot within ten years of marriage. That's compared to 29 percent of women whose parents stayed married.

SHOULD PARENTS STAY TOGETHER FOR THE SAKE OF THE KIDS?
If it's not working, 62 percent of people say cut the cord compared to 33 percent who say stick it out. Compare that to 1981 when 21 percent said the parents should stick together and 71 percent said they shouldn't.

ARE YOU IN A BAD RELATIONSHIP BUT MAKING NO EFFORT TO GET OUT OF IT?
Perhaps one in ten people in relationships are in denial, making excuses for a partner's disappointing and bad behavior. Many believe that if this relationship ends, they'll never find another. Other key reasons for sticking it out include kids and finances.

DID YOU DIVORCE AND RECONNECT?
The odds are in your favor. More than half (54 percent) of divorcés remarry within five years.

WHAT'S THE PRIME REASON TO BREAK UP?
For women it's infidelity (30 percent) and for men, that they've simply grown apart (40 percent vs. 29 percent of women). For 23 percent of men and 27 percent of women, commitment problems played a key role, while 23 percent of men and 17 percent of women

blame insufficient passion. One in four women and 10 percent of men chalk it up to physical or emotional abuse.

WOULD YOU END IT IF YOUR PARTNER HAD A ONE-NIGHT STAND?

Six out of ten women (62 percent) would pack it in if their partner strayed for a one-nighter. Two out of three would call it off if they discovered that their partners had been unfaithful for a while.

AND IF YOUR PARTNER SLEPT WITH SOMEONE OF THE SAME SEX?

Sleeping with another of the same sex seems to be more of a deal-breaker than heterosexual infidelity. Eighty-two percent say they'd pull the plug.

WOULD YOU FORGIVE A SECRET PILE OF PORN MOVIES?

While they may be surprised by it, four out of five women would excuse a secret stash of blue movies and a stockpile of *Penthouse*s under the bed.

IS YOUR MOTHER-IN-LAW A PROBLEM?

Nine out of ten (90 percent) say their mother-in-law is a bone of contention bigger than a brontosaurus's femur.

WHAT WOULD YOU DO IF YOUR PARTNER WHISPERED A FORMER LOVER'S NAME DURING SEX?

While it's not exactly a compliment or turn-on, 52 percent of both men and women say they would forgive their partners this utterance delivered in a fit of passion, though they admit their suspicions and misgivings would be aroused.

WOULD YOU FORGIVE VERBAL ABUSE? HOW ABOUT PHYSICAL?

Half of spouses say they would terminate a relationship if their partner abused them verbally. Almost all (88 percent) would break things off if the abuse turned physical.

CAN BAD SEX TRIGGER A BREAKUP?

While people are loath to admit that being incompatible in bed can dissolve a love bond, in fact one in four relationships that broke up did so because of it. Some decide that their partners are either too stupid or too selfish to love based on bad sex.

IS IT OKAY IF YOUR PARTNER IS CONSISTENTLY LATE MEETING YOU?

It seems women are more forgiving here. Sixty percent would let it roll off their backs but 60 percent of men would be sufficiently miffed to do something about it.

IS IT OKAY IF YOUR PARTNER DOESN'T CALL WHEN HE SAYS HE WILL?

Things come up, we all know, that make it difficult to stick to a plan. That's why 68 percent of women and 65 percent of men forgive their partners when they don't call at the time they said they would.

WHAT ABOUT IF YOUR PARTNER LIES TO YOU?

Surprise: eighty percent of women and 84 percent of men say they can overlook that as well.

IS IT OKAY IF YOUR PARTNER IS INCOMMUNICATIVE?

Depending on the degree of incommunicativeness, 69 percent of women and 79 percent of men claim they wouldn't say anything and would just give their partners space to work it out.

WOULD YOU BE MIFFED IF YOUR PARTNER BLEW YOU OFF TO SPEND TIME WITH FRIENDS?

Half of men would be peeved and the other half understanding. Women are more forbearing: 64 percent say they would look the other way.

HOW ABOUT IF YOUR PARTNER GAVE YOU A THOUGHTLESS GIFT?

Amazingly, 68 percent of women and 70 percent of men say this is sufficient provocation to speak up—and perhaps even break up.

WHAT IF YOU HAD MAJOR DIFFERENCES RAISING THE KIDS?

Almost a quarter (22 percent) say they would go their separate ways if they had serious differences in raising their children. More relevant is the age of the kids, and their economic status and independence.

CAN YOU HANDLE THE SNORING?

One in four cohabiting couples said their sex lives were ruined by snoring and another 40 percent complain that it has caused a lot of nasty arguments.

HOW ABOUT HIS PROPENSITY TO NOD OFF RIGHT AFTER SEX?

One in three women carp that their partners fall asleep immediately after coitus, just when they're ready to talk and cuddle. But rather than view it as a major grievance, most accept it as a fact of life.

WHAT'S THE MAIN CAUSE OF STRESS IN YOUR RELATIONSHIP?

Money is the main source of marital tension for one in four of us. Not sharing the housework irritates 13 percent, and problems with relatives and in-laws grieve 9 percent. Spending money without telling a partner first was the key financial flashpoint.

ARE YOU IRKED THAT YOUR PARTNER ISN'T MORE ROMANTIC?

While it may not be a grating pain, a third of people wish their partners were more romantic. Fifteen percent wish he or she were in the mood more often; 13 percent wish he or she were in the mood less often.

DO YOU WISH YOUR PARTNER WERE MORE ADVENTUROUS?

Eight percent yearn for their partners to be more daring and exploratory. The same percent is slightly ticked off by their lovers' lack of lovemaking skills.

ARE YOU MIFFED AT YOUR LOVER'S BODY?

Seven percent admit they wish their partners had better silhouettes.

WOULD YOU STAY WITH A GUY WHO DRESSED IN YOUR CLOTHES?

Fifty-three percent of women are willing to stay with their fellows, even if it meant they had to share a wardrobe. Some 13 percent of men have admitted to trying on a bra, mostly for fancy dress or a dare, but also for curiosity or pleasure. Most say they found it uncomfortable.

WOULD YOU STAY WITH YOUR FELLOW IF HE ROBBED A BANK?

Fifty-nine percent would remain loyal if their partners participated in some nonviolent crime. Far fewer would stand by their man if he were a murderer.

HAVE YOU EVER HAD SEX TO RESOLVE AN ARGUMENT?

While most of us consider it counterproductive, 22 percent have indeed been turned on by fury and acted on it. Some even go to it *during* an argument, perhaps fired up by seeing their partners with so much intensity.

HOW DO YOU TYPICALLY RESOLVE A FIGHT WITH YOUR PARTNER?

For 48 percent it's a process that entails a period of stewing and then discussing the problem. Another 34 percent talk it out immediately. Five percent say that more often than not, they end up giving in and apologizing. Two percent say they make love to sweep it under the rug.

AFTER A BIG FIGHT DO YOU SERVE UP THE S.T. (SILENT TREATMENT)?

A big fight often ends in prolonged silence. Almost a third of husbands and wives (31 percent) say they stop talking to their mates for an hour or so, and 21 percent are tight-lipped for at least a day. Just 21 percent say they get over it after five minutes or so, while 3 percent keep it up for a week or more. Three out of four people have had a loved one "disappear them," avoiding eye contact or conversation in a passive-aggressive attempt to exert control and make them feel worthless.

HAVE YOU EVER SLEPT APART FROM YOUR MATE OVER A SPAT?

The spare bedroom sofa sure gets a workout. Thirty-six percent of women say they've carted their pillows into another room to punish their offending mate.

HAVE YOU EVER THROWN A SHOE AT YOUR MATE IN ANGER?

Shoes, plates, you name it, it's been hurled. Some 39.5 percent of women admit they've been so peeved at a partner that they've taken aim and let fly.

HAVE YOU EVER PHONED JUST TO SAY SORRY?

Some 51 percent of partners has never phoned to apologize. In fact, 41 percent admit they have used the phone to launch an argument. Sixty-nine percent say a partner has hung up the phone on them in anger—and 13 percent have ended a relationship on the phone.

WHAT GIFT MOST SAYS "I'M SORRY"?

Forty-nine percent would give flowers or houseplants to get out of the doghouse and one in ten think jewelry would do the trick. Eight percent say tickets to an event should soothe the savage beast.

HAVE YOU EVER FORGOTTEN YOUR ANNIVERSARY?

Fully 16 percent of us have forgotten our wedding anniversaries, with 22 percent of men and 11 percent of women guilty as charged. Westerners had the greatest memory lapse: 22 percent forgot the big day, while only 12 percent of northeasterners have. Newlyweds (five years or less) and those making under fifteen thousand a year were least likely to forget.

WHAT'S THE BIGGEST PET PEEVE IN SHARING A BATHROOM?

Two out of five (38 percent) are totally peeved by their partners' refusal to clean the john. Twenty-six percent are irked by the amount of time the other spends in there and 18 percent by their partners' failure to put on a new roll of toilet paper when the old one runs out—or is about to. Twelve percent are fuming that their partners smell up the bathroom and 8 percent by their hogging it with lengthy baths or showers.

DO YOU ARGUE OVER THE REMOTE?

Half of us go at it about the remote. A third are miffed that their partners constantly flip the channels and a fifth (19 percent) that their mate is always losing the damn thing. An equal number (19 percent) argue about who controls it and 4 percent that the other is messing up the settings. Two percent of couples argue that they have too many remotes.

DO YOU FIGHT OVER CLEANING?

Opposites may attract, but not in the laundry room. According to the Soap and Detergent Association, almost half of all couples fight about cleaning and one in ten has broken up over it. Most of the heat occurs over who should do what, how often, and who does it best.

DO YOU EVER ARGUE OVER THE LAUNDRY?

You bet. Nineteen percent say they get into a row over who'll do it. Eight percent each complain about the way it's scattered on the floor and not deposited in the hamper, or about folding clothes. Seven percent are irked by technique—that their partners mix whites and darks—and 6 percent by their partners' lack of follow-through. Five percent clash about items left in pockets or that their partners create too much laundry.

HOW HARD IS BREAKING UP TO DO?

Obviously it depends on what emotional chips you have invested, but judging by the top post-breakup activities, it's harder on women. They're likelier to cry, call friends, listen to a CD, and watch TV in that order. Men are likelier to get physical—ride a bike or go to the gym, listen to a CD, watch TV, and call friends in that order. Twelve percent of men and women confess they'd likely go on a date with somebody else within six hours after the breakup. Men would rather get drunk than call their parents after a breakup. Men are almost equally likely to get drunk as they are to cry after a breakup.

WHO USUALLY ENDS THE RELATIONSHIP?

Women are more likely than men to say that breaking up is hard to do but on the other hand, they're the ones who initiate most breakups. Half of women (51 percent) claim to have initiated their most recent split, interestingly, only 32 percent of men say their partners dumped them; 29 percent say that they were the ones who called it quits; an additional 38 percent say their most recent break-ups were mutually agreed upon by both parties. Only 28 percent of women report that their most recent breaks were mutual.

WHEN DID YOU BREAK UP?

Winter seems to be the most treacherous season for romance: 38 percent of singles say that's the season when their last relationship capsized. Summer and fall tie as the second most vulnerable time, with spring as the season of sanctity.

HOW LONG DO MOST RELATIONSHIPS LAST?

Just like that new car smell, the new person thrill starts to wear off after a few months. The three-month mark is when relationship experts say most new relationships dissolve.

WHERE DO YOU MOST OFTEN STAGE THE BREAKUP?

Hollywood has it nailed. Locations that are both public but fairly private, with a convenient escape route get the nods. Walking in a park is the most popular breakup scenario—public enough to avoid a big scene, but sufficiently intimate. A party or on the job are the worst places to break up, trumped only by being dumped in front of people you see regularly.

WHAT'S THE HARDEST PART ABOUT BREAKING UP?

Both sexes indicated that running into an ex with his or her new romantic partner was the second most difficult situation they faced in the aftermath of a breakup. The first is loneliness and feeling adrift in starting a new life. Four percent say the hardest part of breaking up is getting back their stuff.

WHEN BREAKING UP, DO YOU PREFER THE HARSH TRUTH OR A GENTLE WHITE LIE?

Roll up your sleeves. More than half (53 percent) opt for the painful, unvarnished truth over a confectionary letdown.

WHEN A RELATIONSHIP ENDS, DO YOU OFTEN TAKE THE BLAME?

Women much more than men run the "if I only" line over and over in their heads. As many as three out of four people who've been fired from their relationships wonder would the outcome have been different if they had been more of that, or less of this.

HAVE YOU EVER PLEADED FOR ANOTHER CHANCE?

A third of men and women admit to at least once shamelessly begging a partner who has broken up with them to reconsider and take them back.

HAVE YOU EVER CREATED AN OPPORTUNITY TO MAKE YOUR EX JEALOUS?

Just over 60 percent of those who have been dumped admit they've hit the gym or cosmetician or shown up with a new partner where they knew their former lover would be in the vain hope of waking him or her up to what he or she has cast aside.

HAVE YOU EVER EXACTED REVENGE?

Maybe you haven't gone so far as to have mailed her a week-old fish, your dirty socks, or a prune bouquet, but just over one in five of us admit that we have done some nonviolent vindictive act. Then again, 15 percent of homicides are crimes of passion.

WHAT DO YOU DO TO HEAL A BROKEN HEART?

For 43 percent, recovery often begins with a call to a dear friend or family member, while 29 percent have rented movies or hunkered down in front of the TV. A third begin to look for someone new to date and 22 percent pour themselves a steep one. Fifteen percent admit they try to negate the pain by shopping and one in ten sign up for a vacation. Men are much more likely than women to cope by dating someone new or getting drunk, while women find cleaning, shopping, and writing in a journal to be therapeutic.

DO YOU TEND TO SLEEP MORE AFTER A BREAKUP?

Twenty-two percent of men and 28 percent of women say they find comfort in dreams. On the other hand, 17 percent of men and 22 percent of women say they tend to sleep less in the aftermath of a breakup.

WOULD YOU GO BACK TO YOUR EX-PARTNER FOR SEX?

Forty-two percent say yes, if they are both up front about claiming it's not a new beginning. But 12 percent say they would do so for exactly that purpose: to try to win him or her back. One in five approves if it helps bring about the needed closure. Only 23 percent say no way, that they parted for a reason and that it would be confusing. Some fret it will reignite the painful feelings of rejection. Almost one in four (24 percent) have had sex with a former lover at least once for old times' sake.

WOULD YOU PICK UP AGAIN WITH A PAST LOVE?

Sixty-two percent of people would consider getting back together with a past love.

WOULD YOU APPROVE OF YOUR PARTNER MAINTAINING A RELATIONSHIP WITH HIS OR HER EX?

Some 43 percent profess confidence in their current status, open-mindedness, and an acceptance that everyone has a past and some elements of it can still be enjoyed. One in four admits to mixed feelings—rational and emotional tugs. Twenty-one percent say hang up and cut the cord and 9 percent say they don't want to know about it.

WOULD YOU BE IRKED IF A GOOD FRIEND STARTED DATING YOUR EX?

You bet. Almost three out of four of us (71 percent) admit that just because the relationship has ended, proprietary feelings for the other have not. The rest are more nonchalant, accepting the fact that it's time to move on. If a casual friend started dating an ex, 13 percent would try to get over their upset and reestablish a friendship. Thirty percent would work on being happy they found each other and another 30 percent would avoid speaking with either one.

23

Turn-ons

To each his own, of course. But there are some universal truths about what excites those flames.

BOOBS, BOTTOMS, LIPS, OR THIGHS: WHAT'S THE BIGGEST TURN-ON?

Wherever you go around the world, breasts and bottoms are the biggest turn-on. Forty-seven percent of people regard them as the sexiest body parts. The Chinese like rumps best (93 percent); the Italians least (39 percent). While the world is fractured over lips, eyes, and thighs, there's consensus that the least sexy body parts are the feet.

LEAN AND MEAN OR PLUMP AND RUMP: WHAT'S A BIGGER TURN-ON?

A fuller figure is more likely to set men's pulses racing than a svelte one. *Celebrity Bodies* magazine editor Alison Hall says thinness may look good in clothes and on the runway but not in the sack. Forty-five percent of men prefer full-figured women, 35 percent, an athletic build, and 24 percent, a very slim line.

DO ROMANTIC MOVIES GET YOU GOING?
There's a reason they call them chick flicks. More than twice as many women (27 percent) get romantically attuned from the big screen as men (12 percent). In fact, more than half of those who watched a romance become passionate versus 22 percent who've just watched a macho movie, like *Rambo* or *Die Hard*. Even so, a third of men would only go to see a chick flick under duress and more than one in five would refuse to go at all.

HOW ABOUT A BARBECUE?
Perhaps grilled meat is an exciting throwback to their Neanderthal past, bringing out the caveman spirit, but more than a third of men find barbecues a form of foreplay. Nearly four in ten men muse about sex when, tongs in hand, they prod pieces of meat over the charcoal fire. For one in ten, preparing an alfresco meal is a major turn-on. Three in five women are also aroused by the testosterone-charged atmosphere on the patio.

HOW ABOUT FOOTBALL?
Surprise! Watching football could be good for a man's sex life—providing his team wins. Research from Georgia State University showed levels of testosterone increased by more than 25 percent in guys who watched their side win. Here's the rub: they declined the same amount for those who witnessed their team's defeat.

AND IN THE SUPERMARKET?
Men prefer the hot tub but selecting certain foods is an aphrodisiac for women. More feel romantic shopping for dessert (28 percent) than anywhere else in the store. Other sensual selections: shampoo and similar personal items (18 percent). Even one in one hundred gets excited shopping for canned goods.

DO TAN LINES TURN YOU ON?
Why in the world do people sunbathe in the nude? Four out of ten women and 52 percent of men find tan lines sexually alluring.

WHAT KICKS THINGS OFF ABOUT LEGS?

If you have a foot fetish, you're spending time at the wrong end of the leg. Fifty-three percent of men find a woman's thigh the sexiest part of her leg, while 29 percent vote for the calf. Women flip it: 41 percent view the calf as sexiest, and 18 percent, the thigh. Both genders find the ankle more alluring than the toes. Alas, half of women and men don't consider their own legs sexy.

IS IT SEXIER TO WEAR SOMETHING OR NOTHING AT ALL?

Something, although make sure it's not too much. Forty-three percent of men would rather their partner wear a sexy something or other during their lovemaking. Their top three choices: teddy, stockings, and stilettos.

WHAT'S THE SEXIEST UNDERWEAR FOR GUYS?

Boxers are out of the box. Sixty-three percent of women prefer their guys in them followed by 22 percent who'd rather their fellas wear boxer briefs. Fifteen percent collectively like men in briefs, in French bikinis, or without underwear at all.

AND FOR A GAL?

Thongs are the crowd pleaser: 57 percent of men prefer their partners wear them. Twenty-nine percent opt for bikini underwear. Nine percent would rather their mate go bare-assed and 5 percent find briefs beguiling.

GUYS, PENIS APART, WHERE ELSE SHOULD THEY PLAY?

For 34 percent of men, massaging their nipples is a surefire turn-on and for 29 percent, their necks. Fifteen percent get excited by titillation of their backs and shoulders, and 13 percent, of their earlobes. Two percent are turned on by attention to their hands and feet and 1 percent to the backs of their knees.

DO YOU GET OFF ON WATCHING THE PENIS ENTER THE VAGINA?

Some 73 percent of women and 88 percent of men do. The rest either haven't peeked, or haven't been stimulated by what they saw.

WHAT'S SEXIER: SUIT, SLACKS, OR JEANS?

By a wide margin, 52 percent of women prefer men in denim jeans and casual shirts than any other garb. Thirty-one percent would rather see their fellows in casual slacks and sweaters while 17 percent find suits most intoxicating.

WOULD YOU RATHER YOUR LADY LOVE HAVE LONG OR SHORT HAIR?

They say guys like long hair. Believe it: 53 percent say they prefer cascading locks, while 39 percent like medium-length hair, and 6 percent like it bobbed short.

A TOMBOY OR GIRLY GIRL?

Seventy-one percent of men prefer frills to spills. For all the jokes lobbed at women about their passion for shopping, 78 percent of men would prefer they indulge themselves at the mall than take to the football field.

A GOOD GIRL OR NICE ONE?

The double standard is alive and well. Seven out of 10 men prefer their female partners to be good, although they much appreciate the experience they've received at the hands (or legs) of nice ones. And 61 percent would rather the girl they bring home to Mom be a daddy's girl, adored by her poppa, than a hard-core rebel.

ARE YOU TURNED ON BY PIERCED EARLOBES? A PIERCED NOSE?

Some 47 percent of men and women find pierced earlobes sexy but only 18 percent consider a ring through the nose alluring. Similarly only 18 percent find a pierced tongue appetizing.

DO YOU FIND A PIERCED BELLY BUTTON SEXY? PIERCED NIPPLES?

Forty-three percent of lovers are wowed by the pierced belly button of their partners but only 38 percent of adults find pierced nipples a turn-on. Twenty-one percent consider a pierced labia sexy.

AND IF YOUR PARTNER SHAVED HIS OR HER PUBIC HAIR?

Better check first before you get out the razor. While 47 percent of women say it would get their juices flowing, another 44 percent would be horror-struck. The idea is considerably more provocative to guys: 43.5 percent imagine they'd be really turned on by it, whereas just 11 percent express revulsion.

ARE NIPPLES VISIBLE UNDER A T-SHIRT TANTALIZING?

It may also be tasteless. Forty-six percent of men find this a real turn-on, while another 39 percent find it both tantalizing and tasteless. Fifteen percent are totally turned off by it.

WOULD YOU BE TURNED ON BY YOUR PARTNER MASTURBATING?

Amen and go to it, say 56 percent of men. Another 26 percent figure they'd be awkward initially, but are intrigued by the prospect and expect they'd learn something. For 11 percent, the experience would be a turnoff. Seven percent expect they'd feel hurt and even threatened.

DO YOU ENJOY HAVING AN EROTIC PIC OR TWO OF YOUR HONEY?

Forty-nine percent of women and 70 percent of men would treasure a forbidden photo. For one in five women and 8 percent of men it does nothing—or nothing in their lovers' favor.

ARE YOU TURNED ON BY OTHER COUPLES KISSING AND CUDDLING IN PUBLIC?

The power of suggestion is strong. Fifty-two percent of voyeurs find watching others go at it exhilarative. On the other hand, 48 percent take offense. Similarly only 26 percent of people consider couples who call each other cutesy names in public to be an ear-sore.

WOULD YOU CONSIDER GETTING MARRIED IN LAS VEGAS?

Tacky! Three out of four people consider tying the knot in that gambling mecca to be beyond tasteless.

WOULD YOU LIKE TO GET A VALENTINE'S LOVE NOTE PRINTED IN THE NEWSPAPER?

Three out of five of us would be flattered to read the public notice. But over a third would be put off by a marriage proposal on TV, in skywriting, or any other public venue. This is, after all, an intimate moment.

WOULD WATCHING ANOTHER COUPLE HAVE SEX TURN YOU ON?

Almost twice as many men as women say it definitely would get their juices going (43 percent vs. 24 percent) and they'd hop to it if they had the chance. Twenty-one percent of women say that while it might excite them they'd never actually do it, whereas 19 percent of men would like to try and 14.5 have already done it.

WHAT ABOUT WATCHING TWO WOMEN GOING AT IT?

Seventy-two percent of women admit, some sheepishly, that they are or would be intrigued by this. So would 91 percent of men.

HOW ABOUT THE IDEA OF HAVING SEX WITH A VIRGIN?

For 37 percent of men this is nirvana, while for another 38 percent it's pretty heady stuff. Another 5.4 percent would be turned off. It wouldn't do much for 56 percent of women either but 26 percent admit they'd find that a welcome prospect.

HOW ABOUT IF YOUR PARTNER STRIPPED FOR YOU—WITH ALL THE HOOPLA?

No wonder *The Full Monty* won such acclaim. Only 17 percent of women wouldn't like such a tease, or would find it ridiculous. Even fewer men (6.1 percent) would object.

DOES NIBBLING, LICKING, AND KISSING YOUR EARS AROUSE YOU?

Eighty-three percent of men and women like or love being nibbled and licked. Fifteen percent of women and 8 percent of men are impassive, including 8.2 percent of women and 3.5 percent of men actively turned off by it.

HOW ABOUT BEING BITTEN DURING SEX?

No hurtful Dracula stuff but 79 percent of women and 71 percent of men crave those love bites in varying degrees of strength.

DO YOU ENJOY HAVING YOUR NIPPLES STIMULATED WHEN YOU'RE AROUSED?

It's an absolute go for almost twice as many women as men (61.3 percent vs. 31.4 percent). But 10 percent of women and 12.6 percent of men find it irritating.

IS IT EXCITING WHEN YOUR PARTNER GROANS WHILE HAVING SEX?

Two out of three men and 56 percent of women get turned on by a partner, who moans, groans, grunts, and snorts. For the rest, those noisy emissions must come at the right time or they can be comical or off-putting.

WHAT IF YOUR PARTNER TURNED PASSIVE DURING SEX?

Three out of five women and 70 percent of men say they'd hasten to get down to business to make up for their passive partner. But 7.1 percent of women and 8.8 percent of men would worry that they weren't pleasuring their partner sufficiently, and another third of women and 22 percent of men would feel hesitant, bored, intimidated, unloved, or angry at their partner.

WHAT'S THE MOST ROMANTIC THING YOUR MATE COULD DO FOR YOU?

They could send flowers (31 percent) or serve breakfast in bed (29 percent) but in this pedal-to-the metal world, the real romantic overture is doing some household chores so their partner can get an extra hour of sleep (37 percent).

WHAT'S SEXY: FINGERS THROUGH HAIR, SMILING?

Apparently nothing says sexy better than a smile. Sixty-two percent of men and 48 percent of women find it the most appealing gesture in a member of the opposite sex. After a smile, women found the act of holding a door open to be the most appealing gesture in a man

(43 percent), while one in five men found a woman running her fingers through her hair tantalizing.

HOW ABOUT CROSSED LEGS?
Nearly half of U.S. women (45 percent) cross their legs almost all the time, often out of habit but also as a way of flirting. Just 21 percent of men adopt this default position. Seventy percent of men and 47 percent of women think leg-crossing is flirtatious and looks sexy.

IS PERFUME OR COLOGNE A TURN-ON?
Most men and women don't care but 40 percent of men claim to be flattered if a partner wears perfume. Vanilla is the spice that sends more women's pulses racing, but most men prefer citrus. However, fewer than one in five men use vanilla-scented lotion or aftershave.

IS A BALD PATE SEXY?
Women are of two minds on this one. Half rate bald men as sexy, though few men losing their hair find solace here.

ARE SPECTACLES A TURN-ON OR -OFF?
Forty-five percent of men think that glasses make a woman look sexy, while 28 percent say women wearing specs look more intelligent than those without.

DO YOU FIND EXERCISE A TURN-ON?
Two out of three runners reported increased sexual vigor, and four out of five feel more sexually confident. But too much of a good thing can be bad. More than half of those who run at least 30 miles a week are sometimes too tired for sex (compared with only a third of those who run less). In swimming, the turning point seems to be three days a week, 45 minutes a day. Heavy training—swimming 18 hours or more a week—deadens sexual desire.

24

Turnoffs

There's an axiom in the world of marketing and customer relations that it's at least five times more expensive to acquire a new customer as it is to retain one you've already got. So be very careful not to alienate any. This advice holds for the world of love relationships. Turn someone off and he or she can be good as gone.

WHAT'S THE BEST WAY TO TURN SOMEONE OFF?
Talk about your ex. That's a surefire way, both men and women agree, to suppress a partner's ardor in the early stages of a romance. Almost three out of five women say a guy who brings up a former girlfriend on a first date means there will be no second date.

DO "TONSIL MINERS" WHO KISS IN PUBLIC DISGUST YOU?
Most men (51 percent) and women (59 percent) consider a quick peck appropriate, but longer than thirty seconds is disturbing to most. Americans don't view themselves prudish but PDAs (public displays of affection, not personal digital assistants) make them itchy.

HOW MUCH OF A TURNOFF IS POOR POSTURE?
Doesn't have to be the hunchback of Notre Dame; even slumped shoulders deflate 63 percent of us.

HOW ABOUT A SOUR PUSS?
Three out of five people say they'd be hard-pressed to enter a long-term relationship with someone who rarely smiles and two out of three declare it would preclude them pursuing even a short-term relationship.

HOW ABOUT A CHEAPSKATE?
By a 60 percent majority, women would rather date a man who's a so-so lover than one who's cheap.

HOW ABOUT SOMEONE WHO IS CLOSE-MOUTHED? OR TOO OPEN-MOUTHED?
More than three out of five people would rule out a long-term relationship with someone who safeguards his opinions as if they were the royal jewels. More than 43 percent find this trait sufficiently unattractive to scuttle a short-term connection. On the other hand, four out of five women are put off by vulgar language.

HOW DO YOU FEEL ABOUT BODY HAIR?
A lot of hair on the torso turns off 37.2 percent of women—and turns on 16.4 percent of them. As for a woman's hirsute legs or armpits, 72 percent of men find them a definite downer, while 4 percent say they appreciate their partners in a natural state. Hair in unwanted places on a partner offends more than twice as many people as do rolls of fat around the middle.

WHAT'S A BIGGER BUMMER: BAD BREATH OR PASSIVITY?
Don't just lie there! More than half of people (55 percent) find a mate who just lies there to be a real spoiler. Only 26 percent find bad breath the ultimate assault. But don't get lazy about oral hygiene. People rank bad breath as just about 2.5 times more offensive than body odor.

WOULD YOU BE TURNED OFF IF YOUR PARTNER PIERCED HIS OR HER GENITALS?

A word to the wise: don't do it. Fifty-seven percent of women and half of men say they'd be either totally revolted or not very enthusiastic about seeing anything punctured down there. Just 15 percent of men and 11 percent of women would find it provocative. Navel and toe rings are also unwelcome, though the former significantly more than the latter.

WHICH WOULD PUT YOU OFF SEX FASTER: TAXES OR JURY DUTY?

Call in the IRS. Three out of five of us (59 percent) say filing their taxes is more of a sex dampener than serving on jury duty.

DO YOU PREFER DIRTY LAUNDRY OR DIRTY TALK?

Dirty laundry is grosser than dirty talk for 72 percent of us. And 62 percent consider dirty secrets a bigger relationship damager than dirty pictures.

HOW ABOUT NO SENSE OF HUMOR? POOR CONVERSATION SKILLS?

Sixty-three percent of singles say that a tin ear and dull wit can short-circuit a courtship—even more than the 56 percent who consider an inability to hold up his or her end of the conversation to be a deal-breaker.

HOW ABOUT POOR TABLE MANNERS? CHRONIC LATENESS? FORGETFULNESS? CELLPHONE USE?

Slurping soup, elbows on the table, these are definite no-nos for half of us. Forty-one percent of people could not forgive routine tardiness in a partner. And 23 percent consider that a mind like a sieve is too great an albatross to carry in a relationship. Leave the cellphone at home: three out of five people smolder when their date receives a cell call—and takes it.

WHAT IF YOUR DATE HAD OPPOSITE TASTES IN MUSIC, MOVIES, BOOKS, ETC.?

While a difference of opinion is exciting, different strokes sometimes make for different swimming holes. Seventeen percent say radically different tastes in life's pleasures can make for a lot of lonely sulking. Twelve percent could not tolerate clashing political views.

HOW DO YOU FEEL ABOUT A DATED WARDROBE? BAD HAIRCUT?

Sixteen percent wouldn't want to be seen with someone in a lame getup. And a Mohawk, mullet, or other motley mess of hair eliminates 15 percent of prospects.

WHAT'S THE WORST SENSE TO OFFEND?

Better you should look like a drip than smell like a swamp. Seventy-nine percent of women warn that their olfactory sense is not to be messed with. More than four out of five would never invite a guy who smelled bad to get between their sheets.

25

Valentine's Day

They call *this* a holiday for lovers? Valentine's Day is thought to be named after St. Valentine who was martyred for his faith. Others connect it to an early Roman festival, Lupercalia, at which men whipped women with animal hides to make them fertile. A less gruesome possible basis for the lovers' holiday is an old English legend that this is when birds pick mates. Either way, in modern times it's a marketing must. Do you celebrate?

DOES THE FEBRUARY FOURTEENTH SPIRIT MOVE YOU?

More than three out of four of us (77 percent) give gifts and cards on this holiday of love, but two thirds have no idea why it's called Valentine's Day or how the whole event got started. Two out of every three of us call ourselves romantics and celebrate the occasion. Thirty-eight percent dine out and 12 percent share a romantic dinner at home. One in ten see a movie, play, or concert. Five percent take a romantic getaway. Just 28 percent don't celebrate, including one in four who find it all depressing.

WHAT DO YOU USUALLY GIVE OR GET?

One in five receives chocolate or candy. Thirty-two percent send flowers. Three percent unwrap lingerie and 11 percent, clothes. Stuffed animals are big, with 18 percent bringing one home and 11 percent buying perfume or cologne. Eighteen percent bestow jewelry: men are three times more likely to give jewelry than women.

DO YOU SAY IT WITH FLOWERS?

While 64 percent of floral purchases this time of year are made by men, one in five women sends flowers to her partner. And 15 percent send flowers to themselves, perhaps to suggest amour or make themselves feel loved. Roses are chosen by the greatest number of flower-buyers, with red the preferred choice, followed by pink, peach, yellow, and then a mix of colors. Seventy percent of women prefer to receive their flowers at the office.

WHAT DO YOU TYPICALLY SPEND ON A VALENTINE'S DAY GIFT?

It seems men are the ones from Venus. In a recent year they spent an average $107 for Valentine's Day gifts compared to the $46 by women. Collectively that came to an average $77.43 shelled out for Valentine's Day gifts. Almost 60 percent of people consider the day as too expensive; three-quarters call the holiday overmarketed.

GUYS, DO YOU DREAD VALENTINE'S DAY OR HAPPILY ANTICIPATE IT?

"Dread" is the word. More than half of women think men get antsy about this day of romance and 38 percent of men agree. Only 29 percent of women think men look forward to it. In fact, 42 percent of men say they do.

WHO RECEIVES THE MOST VALENTINE'S GIFTS?

Women do. Almost three of every four women expect to receive a little something for Valentine's Day versus 59 percent of men. In general, spouses, children, and parents clean up the most in that order, followed by girlfriends/boyfriends and friends. In last place? The boss.

WHO GETS THE MOST VALENTINE'S CARDS?

Teachers draw better than lovers on this count, but then so do children (number two) and spouses (number three). Lovers are in fourth place followed by friends and other relatives. Americans send a billion cards each Valentine's Day, second only to Christmas. A third of the cards accompany gifts. Romantic cards are the bestsellers, but 25 percent are humorous.

WHICH WOULD YOU RATHER RECEIVE: A FUNNY CARD OR A ROMANTIC ONE?

Humor wins by a landslide with 51 percent of both men and women choosing it. Some 26 percent of men and 35 percent of women would prefer to receive a romantic card, while 13 percent of men and 4 percent of women would opt for a sexy card, according to the International Mass Retail Association.

LADIES, WOULD YOU PREFER GREAT LINGERIE OR A GREAT NOVEL?

Many more women would rather receive really great underwear than receive a really great novel on this occasion.

HOW ABOUT WINE OR SWEETS?

Fifty-nine percent of women would rather their guy show up with a bottle of red or white compared to 41 percent who'd rather have chocolate. The American Boxed Chocolate Manufacturers Association says women's favorite Valentine's Day candy are caramels but men prefer syrupy cherries. After caramels, the most popular chocolates are nuts, cherries, coconut, and solid chocolate.

HOW WOULD YOU FEEL ABOUT RECEIVING SOMETHING, UM, PRACTICAL?

Get with the program. This is a day for frivolity. Although most women won't complain, 23 percent consider practical gifts like everyday clothes or gift certificates to be flat-footed and inappropriate. Fourteen percent of women promise they'd shed the callow fellow who presented them with money on this occasion. On the other hand, Intuit found that 41 percent of women and 38 percent of men would love to receive stock shares on Valentine's Day.

DO YOU WATCH A ROMANTIC MOVIE ON VALENTINE'S DAY?

Assuming you're staying home to celebrate the holiday, more than half curl up with a romantic movie like *Say Anything, Annie Hall, When Harry Met Sally, Four Weddings and a Funeral,* and *Sense and Sensibility.*

WHAT'S THE MOST ROMANTIC MEAL?

Vegetarians are in a pickle. No entrée says romance better than steak, followed by seafood and chicken. Heart-shaped cookies are viewed as the most romantic Valentine's Day dessert, followed by chocolate fondue. Crème brûlée and truffles trail with just 14 and 13 percent of the vote respectively, according to the International Communications Research for Sur La Table.

WHAT'S THE MOST ROMANTIC ICE CREAM FLAVOR?

A Häagen-Dazs Opinion Research Poll determined chocolate was most romantic by a whisker, followed by butter pecan, strawberry, and vanilla Swiss almond.

IS IT TACKY TO PROPOSE ON VALENTINE'S DAY?

More than half of folks consider it too clichéd and cheesy to be meaningful. Eighteen percent think it's the perfect day. Another 42 percent say go with the flow as long as you make the proposal creative. One percent of people have proposed or been proposed to on Valentine's Day. And 58 percent of marrieds would consider it an appropriate day to renew their vows.

DO YOU SHOW LOVE AND APPRECIATION BY BUYING BIG GIFTS?

Three out of five of us deny doing this but 35 percent own up to such crass demonstrations. The rest wonder what qualifies as "big" or what's wrong with it. Thirty-eight percent admit they've gone all out, buying an expensive Valentine's gift to make up for an argument.

DO YOU KNOW THE SIZE OF SOMEONE YOU'RE SHOPPING FOR?

Most women know the collar and inseam size of the person they plan to gift. But only about half of men head to the stores knowing the difference between a size two and size twelve. Perhaps that's why so many Valentine's gifts are flowers, plants, or candy.

WHEN DO YOU SHOP?
Typically most lovebirds make their Valentine's purchases the week before the holiday. Traditionally, around a third of men wait and shop for their gifts the day before.

WHAT'S THE APPROPRIATE RESPONSE FOR A LOVER WHO FORGETS VALENTINE'S DAY?
Only 11 percent figure they'd get very upset and hold a grudge, while 54 percent would be hurt and lay on the guilt trip for ten minutes, then get over it. More than one in four imagine they'd forgive and understand that life is hectic, while 9 percent wave it off as irrelevant: it's just a manufacturer's holiday anyway. And if he didn't forget but gave you nothing? Fifty-three percent of women say they'd drop a guy who turned up empty-handed with no excuse.

HAVE YOU EVER BOUGHT YOURSELF A VALENTINE?
One in nine love missives received on this day were sent by people to themselves to save face, according to Amazon.com.

DO YOU THINK GIVING A GIFT WILL INCREASE YOUR CHANCES OF GETTING SEX?
Eighteen percent of Americans confuse a gift with the first move in foreplay. That includes 29 percent of men and 8 percent of women.

26

All in the Family

Eighty-six percent of folks are satisfied with their familial relationships and many of them define themselves as more than satisfied. Despite two wage-earner households, 19 percent of people think that family ties are closer today than they were in their parents' day.

✗ WHAT'S THE FIRST THING YOU DO WHEN YOU COME HOME?

Four times as many men as women hug their spouses first thing when they walk in the door after work. For most people the first order of business is to kick off their shoes (24 percent). Next most popular: change clothes (20 percent), followed by listening to phone messages (10 percent) and opening the mail (10 percent). The kids, spouses and pets get equal priority: 8 percent head to one of them first. Two percent head to the stove or refrigerator and a few stragglers turn on a TV, computer, or CD player.

HOW OFTEN DO YOU EAT DINNER AT HOME EN FAMILLE?

Despite all the talk about the car replacing the dining room table or living room hearth, half of Americans say they eat dinner at home with their family almost every night. Another 18 percent say they sit down together for a meal several times a week.

DO YOU HAVE A SET PLACE AT THE DINNER TABLE?

Whether the seat was actually assigned is irrelevant; 79 percent of us feel territorial and always sit in the same spot.

DO YOU WATCH TV DURING DINNER?

Some 44 percent of us multitask this way, while 26 percent listen to music and 16 percent to the radio during the meal.

WHEN DID YOU HAVE YOUR FIRST CHILD?

The average age when American mothers give birth to their first child keeps inching up. In 1970 it was 21.4 years and in 1975, 21.8. Five years later it was up to 22.7 and in 1985, 23.7. By 1990 the average first-time birth was to a woman 24.2 years old and in 1995, 24.5. In 2000, the average first-time mom was 24.9 years old.

WHEN DID YOU FIRST FEEL LIKE A DAD?

Three out of four men say they knew they were dads when they first held their wee ones and 7 percent when they began to prefer sleep to sex. For another 4 percent the realization hit when they turned around when another child called "Daddy." Almost a third of guys and 17 percent of women feel that today's dads have gone soft. Lower income folks and southerners are more likely to think today's dads have lost their virility.

ARE YOU CHILD-FREE BY CHOICE?

If you are, you're a member of a growing minority. The number of voluntarily childless couples has grown from 2.4 percent in 1982, and 4.3 percent in 1990, to 6.6 percent in 1998.

HAVE YOU EVER LIED ABOUT YOUR KIDS' AGES TO PAY LESS?

Ever? Twenty-three percent of parents admit they regularly fib about their kids' ages to get them into places for free.

HAVE YOU EVER HAD YOUR KIDS LIE THAT YOU WEREN'T HOME TO AVOID TAKING A CALL?

Forty percent confess they regularly have Junior tell callers to whom they don't want to speak that Mommy's not home.

DO YOU EVER DO YOUR KIDS' HOMEWORK FOR THEM?

There's a reason Jamie got an "A." Thirteen percent of parents *admit* they occasionally do more than guide their offspring; they do the work and pass it off as Junior's.

HOW OFTEN DO YOU HUG YOUR KIDS?

If a hug a day keeps the doctor away we've got one healthy society. Eighty-seven percent of moms and 73 percent of dads claim they hug their kids (under age thirteen) at least once a day. And 85 percent of mothers and 62 percent of fathers tell their child that they love him or her just as often. Fifty-five percent of mothers and 37 percent of fathers tell their child that they appreciate something he or she did.

HOW FAR FROM THE MOTHERLODE DO YOU LIVE?

The tribe thrives. One in ten twenty-five- to thirty-four-year-olds have moved back in and 4 percent of grown-ups live upstairs or down. Eleven percent live within two miles of their parents and 27 percent live within a few hours' drive. The Census counts 3.9 million multigenerational families sharing a household, mainly recent immigrants, out-of-wedlock parents, or those who live where housing is especially scarce or pricey. A third of people live less than a mile from some relative.

HOW NEAR DO YOU *WANT* TO LIVE TO YOUR FAMILY?

When buying a house one in five people look close to where their parents live. And 40 percent claim they'd be happy to have their mothers-in-law stay indefinitely.

HOW OFTEN DO YOU CALL HOME?

Four out of five young adults claim they call to chat with Mom at least once a week and two out of three talk to Dad just as often. Single men are three times as likely as married men to call Mom (42 percent vs. 17 percent). Two-thirds of women think their husbands should only speak to their mothers once a week.

WHERE ARE YOUR SIBLINGS ON YOUR RADAR SCREEN?

We have, on average, one or two sibs. Just 5 percent have never had a brother or sister while 29 percent have had five or more, including stepsiblings. For 7 percent, never is too soon to see or call them. But 44 percent are in touch with at least one sibling at least once a month, and one in five at least twice a week. Twenty-nine percent check in a few times a year, mainly on holidays and special occasions. Eighty percent exchange holiday cards and 75 percent buy each other gifts. Half even spend an occasional vacation with their brothers or sisters.

WOULD YOU MENTION A SIBLING IN YOUR WILL?

We may not see them often, but at death's door we think of them. Nearly one in four people (including 32 percent of forty-five- to fifty-four-year-olds) names a sib in their will, either as guardians for their children, trustees of their money, or executors of the will itself. Sixteen percent name them as beneficiaries of their life insurance policies.

DID YOU SUFFER ABUSE AT THE HANDS OF YOUR SIBS?

Spousal abuse gets all the ink but 65 percent of children with brothers or sisters recall severe physical violence administered by their siblings, such as being choked, pounded with fists, bitten, or kicked. Eight percent said the fights were entirely one-sided. A third claim they were verbally or emotionally abused by a sister or brother. Yet 85 percent say the conflicts were beneficial, teaching them self-control, assertiveness, realistic awareness of self-limits, and their limited ability to control others.

WHO DO YOU LOOK TO FOR HELP WHEN YOU'RE SICK?

Perhaps because we've been conditioned by Mom's ever-comforting presence, more of us look to her when we're under the weather than anyone else. Daughters come in second followed by best friends and sisters. Aging parents look to their sons first for help with heavy chores before they call a friend, brother, or, finally, daughter.

WHO WOULD YOU TAP TO BORROW A BIG SUM?

It seems that when it comes to money, Father knows best, or at least is the easiest mark. After hitting him up, adults would next go to Mom, and then another relative before putting the lean on a best friend.

WHO DO YOU LOOK TO WHEN UPSET WITH YOUR PARTNER?

No one is going to listen the way a close friend will when we're peeved by a mate or depressed. Surprisingly, more people will then talk to a clergyman before telling Mom or another relative about a problem with a partner. But when depression strikes, sisters are next in line as confidantes for most of us followed by Mom and then daughter.

DO YOU CONSIDER MOM YOUR BEST FRIEND?

Nineteen percent of us admit that she has become their best friend. Forty-seven percent say they could even tell Mom she needs to lose weight. Another 22 percent consider their moms great role models. But half say they're on automatic pilot here: they "love" their mothers because they survived raising them and always had dinner on the table and clean clothes in the closet.

WHAT DO YOU USUALLY SPEND FOR MOTHER'S DAY?

Mother's Day is second only to Christmas as a gift-giving holiday. According to International Mass Retail Association and American Greetings, each of us shells out on average about $75 on Mom for the occasion. African Americans and Latinos spend more—on average $100. Eighty percent of us buy a greeting card, making that the top gift followed by flowers, dinner or brunch, gardening gear, clothes, jewelry, and stuff for the house. Some 46 percent of us spread the cheer around, also sending cards and gifts to stepmoms, daughters, grandmothers, godmothers, aunts and even friends who are moms, and 13 percent give gifts to others on this occasion. Thirty-eight percent of men and 24 percent of women plead guilty to at least once forgetting to send Mom a Mother's Day gift or card.

WILL YOU PHONE HOME ON MOTHER'S DAY? EAT OUT?

Whether out of guilt or genuine devotion, more of us call Mom on Mother's Day than any other day of the year. Collectively long-distance phone companies say it rivals Christmas for being the best call-home holiday. It's also the hardest day of the year to get restaurant reservations as four in 10 adults will eat out on Mother's Day. Less than two of 10 adults will eat out on Father's Day.

WHAT DO YOU USUALLY SPEND FOR DAD ON HIS DAY?

Poor Dad. He loses on this front, too. According to International Mass Retail Association and American Greetings, the average American shells out about $50 on Father's Day.

DO YOU HAVE YOUR PARENTS WRAPPED AROUND YOUR PINKIE?

Two-thirds of nine- to seventeen-year-olds claim they generally succeed at getting their parents to do what they want, like buy the snack foods they crave. Forty percent claim they're able to drag Mom and Dad to an eatery that's offering a special toy. But just 38 percent concede they often succeed in persuading their parents to spend more time with them.

DO YOU PLAN THE HOLIDAYS AROUND JUNIOR?

Ninety-three percent of parents plan vacations with the kids' interests in mind, using the holiday to bring them closer together. Given a choice, more than nine out of 10 kids want a best friend to come along. Moms are their second favorite pick, followed by dads. Siblings are who they most want to leave home. Grandparents come along on more than 20 percent of family vacations.

DO YOU FEEL REMORSE IF YOU LEAVE THE LITTLE BUGGERS HOME?

More than two of five parents say they feel guilty if they don't bring their kids along on vacation. Only 27 percent say the hassle trumps remorse.

WHEN BABY MAKES THREE, DOES HE OR SHE SNUGGLE IN YOUR BED?

Some 12.5 percent of families let their infants share their bed, up from 5.8 percent a decade ago, according to the National Institute of Child Health. Blacks are four times as likely as whites to invite the baby in and Asian Americans more likely than Latinos to make room. Nearly half of men and 38 percent of women feel their relationship and sex life suffered when Junior came along.

HAVE YOU EVER ATTENDED A FAMILY REUNION, OTHER THAN THE HOLIDAYS?

Forty-five percent of us have attended a family reunion in this circumstance.

27

You Gotta Have Friends

We've all grown up with the admonition to make new friends but keep the old—one is silver and the other is gold. How rich is your treasury?

HAVE YOU ADJUSTED YOUR "BANK ACCOUNT" LATELY?

Almost half of us (46 percent) have added a silver friend to our banks recently, while 12 percent have jettisoned (or "withdrawn") a long-term golden friendship.

DO YOU HAVE ENOUGH FRIENDS?

Two-thirds of us feel blessed with a trove of good friends in our lives. But one in four don't and miss it acutely. The biggest problem women claim they face when it comes to making new friends is lack of time to nurture a seedling—two times more problematic than lack of opportunities to meet prospects.

HOW MANY FRIENDS IS ENOUGH?

The average Joe or Josephine has no less than 14 close friends. Thirty percent of people have at least five close friends living nearby. On the opposite extreme, 27 percent of people rue that they have no close friends living in their local area. Two-thirds consider their friendship network to be satisfactory; that is, they see or speak to friends at least once a week and have at least one close friend who lives nearby. That's more than the 52 percent who have a satisfactory relatives network. One in five has neither.

DO YOU HAVE A BEST BUD?

Eighty percent can name, without any difficulty, their best friend and most of them claimed to meet up with this special pal at least once a week. The average American has known his or her best friend for fourteen years; two-thirds have been best friends for at least a decade. Thirty-six percent go back at least 20 years. Only 15 percent of adults consider someone they've known for less than five years to be their best friend.

WOULD YOU READILY LOAN YOUR BEST FRIEND A THOUSAND DOLLARS?

Regardless of their financial situation, three out of four best friends (74 percent) say they would always reach in their pocket to provide a little fast cash to a friend in need. Almost three out of four feel they'd put their life on the line for a best friend.

WOULD YOU WANT TO MOVE IN WITH YOUR BEST FRIEND?

We may love them to death but not to live with. Almost half of people say they like their best pals considerably more from afar. Just 56 percent would enjoy rooming together. On the other hand, 91 percent would love to vacation together, with women savoring this even more than men (93 percent vs. 88 percent).

HOW OFTEN DO YOU SEE YOUR BEST FRIEND?

Forty-five percent of adults get together face-to-face with their bosom buddy at least once a week. Sixteen percent see each other daily. Just 27 percent meet less than once a month. But 23 percent talk to them every day with women likelier than men to do so. Seventy-one percent of those under age twenty-five versus half of those sixty-five and older chat with their top buddy at least once a week, and 36 percent phone daily.

WHAT'S THE AVERAGE NUMBER OF FRIENDS YOU SEE REGULARLY?

We may have lots of 'em but we only see four regularly, down from 5.4 a score ago.

HAVE YOU EVER GOTTEN WORK THROUGH A FRIEND?

Thirty-seven percent of people currently working say they got their current job through someone they knew. For one in four of us, it was through a close friend or family member.

HAVE YOU EVER GOTTEN THROUGH WORK BECAUSE OF A FRIEND?

Paycheck aside, what makes workers happy is friendship. Fifty-nine percent say interaction with fellow workers is the highlight of their workday.

HAVE YOU KEPT THE FRIENDS FROM A PREVIOUS WORKPLACE?

You shed the boss and the cubicle but not the pals. Sixty-one percent of Americans who've moved on to a new position have kept the friends they've made at their last job.

IS ANYTHING OFF-LIMITS WHEN YOU AND YOUR PALS TALK?

For 65 percent of solid friendships, nothing is verboten. But 30 percent of women say they won't discuss their sex lives with their friends and one in five won't talk about money.

IS A SISTER OR BROTHER A BEST FRIEND?

Families are the folks you're stuck with, the saying goes, and friends are the ones you pick. But 40 percent of women count a sibling as one of a handful of best friends.

ARE YOUR REALLY CLOSE FRIENDS A LOT LIKE YOU?

Opposites may attract, but not too often as friends. Most people hang with those demographically similar to themselves. Most best friends (73 percent) are within five years of each other's age and more than seven out of ten best friends share the same marital status. Just 17 percent are bosom buddies with someone from a different race and only one in three claim to have at least one close friend whose with a different lifestyle than theirs.

HOW GOOD A FRIEND ARE YOU?

A better friend than lover. Ninety-nine percent of people pat themselves on the back in the friendship arena. They think they're excellent listeners and advisers and they have their friends' interests at heart.

WOULD YOU LET A FRIEND IN A JAM MOVE IN FOR A WHILE?

They say fish and guests smell after three days. But friends, it seems, have a pleasing if not neutral odor. Some 79 percent would lay out the welcome mat, regarding helping a friend in need is a gift to themselves.

HAVE YOU EVER LENT MONEY TO A CLOSE FRIEND?

If you're counting on being repaid, follow Polonius's advice: neither a borrower nor a lender be. Fifty-nine percent of people have loaned money to a friend but only 27 percent were completely paid back. A third of those with lightened wallets swear they'd never do it again.

WOULD YOU DONATE AN ORGAN OR BONE MARROW TO A SICK FRIEND?

It would have to be an awfully close friend but two out of three people say they'd do so.

WOULD YOU TELL A LIE TO SAVE A FRIEND PAIN?

We certainly might tell them their pie was delicious when it wasn't or that no one would notice the blotch on their face, but with something important most of us profess that we cannot tell a lie. A third believe they would tell a humdinger to cover up for a friend or provide an alibi.

IS YOUR MATE OR SIGNIFICANT OTHER YOUR BEST FRIEND?

More than half of us call our husband or wife our best friend. Eighty-one percent claim to be able to talk to them about anything and everything.

DO YOU CONFIDE IN A FRIEND STUFF YOU'VE KEPT FROM YOUR MATE?

Forty-three percent of friends share secrets with each other about which their lovers know nothing.

DID YOU EVER FALL OUT WITH A GOOD FRIEND OVER AN UNFORGIVABLE ACT?

One in five of us have parted ways with someone with whom they were once very close because of something heinous and unexpected that the ex-friend did.

HOW DO YOU STAY IN TOUCH WITH FRIENDS?

The phone is still the instrument of choice. Three out of five of us say we regularly ring up our friends. Surprisingly, meeting at a restaurant and hashing over lives beats out email contact and 17 percent still put pen to paper.

CAN YOU HAVE A PLATONIC FRIENDSHIP?

The French call this cross-sex spiritual or intellectual relationship "aimite en rose." More than a third of men and 15 percent of women call it impossible. Just 18 percent have a close friend of the opposite sex, with young people and singles the most likely candidates. Some 92 percent of women say their best friend is a woman and 88 percent of men say their best friend is another man.

IS TENSION IN A CROSS-SEX FRIENDSHIP INEVITABLE?

Men like it; women don't, but 62 percent of all say sexual tension is present in their cross-sex friendships. Two out of three young people had sex with a friend but fewer than half of those relationships morphed into a romance.

HAVE YOU EVER BETRAYED A FRIEND'S SECRETS?

Despite the blood oath, the secret handshakes, the collateral of a mother's life proffered, 46 percent of friends have spilled the beans on secrets they promised to take to the grave.

WHAT'S MORE IMPORTANT IN A FRIEND: HONESTY OR LOYALTY?

Pets are partial; friends are fair. You count on them for a true assessment and to tell the horse when he has behaved like an ass. Truthfulness and trustworthiness are more important by a four to one margin. But loyalty is the second most important factor followed by a sense of humor. Eighty-eight percent of men and women think their friends would describe them as straight shooters.

WHAT'S MORE IMPORTANT IN A FRIEND: FUN OR KINDNESS?

Fun wins by 60 percent. It also beats out being understanding and a good listener.

HAVE YOU MET ANY FRIENDS ONLINE?

Amazingly, 58 percent of people who use the Net claim they've met someone with whom they've become friends or they've reconnected with an old friend online.

HOW WELL DO YOU KNOW YOUR NEIGHBORS?

While it may be as American as apple pie to talk over the fence or borrow a cup of flour, life in the 'hood is not all wine and roses. Seventeen percent of Americans don't know the people next door at all and few spend much time with them. At the same time, 77 percent of Americans feel connected to their communities, and 28 percent claim to feel *very* connected.

ARE ANY OF YOUR NEIGHBORS FRIENDS?

Three out of four of us call the folks next door friends. Almost as many have been helped out by a neighbor in an emergency.

ARE YOU HAPPY WITH YOUR NEIGHBORS?

Two out of three people think they've landed well, geographically speaking. No surprise, ruralites are a lot more up on who lives nearby than city dwellers. Midwesterners may be the friendliest of all: 62 percent of them know their neighbors well.

WOULD YOU RENEGE ON BUYING A HOUSE BECAUSE OF WHO LIVED NEXT DOOR?

Four out of ten buyers have walked away from buying a property they liked because of unsavory types living next door. The Woolwich First Time Buyers Survey found nearly a third now try to vet neighbors before making an offer.

HAVE YOU EVER FOUGHT WITH A NEIGHBOR?

One in three of us has exchanged frosty words. Nearly half have been ticked off by something the gremlins next door did to their property. One in five of us has been so enraged that she's dialed for police intervention. Three percent have taken some retaliatory measure to something a neighbor did that offended them. Fifteen percent have eavesdropped on a neighbor's private conversation.

WHAT PULLS YOUR CHAIN MOST ABOUT A NEIGHBOR?

Robert Frost said good fences make good neighbors. The mute button improves relations even more. For 36 percent the noise neighbors make rattles them most, and for 32 percent each, it's unruly kids and pets. One in four complain that neighbors don't return what they borrow and that they're messy, perhaps decreasing the value of their own homes. Sixteen percent are put off by a neighbor's cold shoulder and 7 percent by when they mow the lawn. Five percent are miffed by neighbors who are *too* friendly.

DO YOU RUSH OVER TO WELCOME THE NEIGHBORHOOD NEWBIES?

That's why there are organized welcome wagons. Just 14 percent of neighbors would give a newcomer cookies or pay a visit. Fifty-nine percent would wait to see the neighbor outside before saying hello to them and one in five would only give a casual wave and smile in passing.

28

Sex Sells

Lipstick magnate Charles Revson once said he wasn't selling lip color as much as hope. Indeed, sex, or the suggestion of it, has been used to push everything from toothpaste to dungarees, to cars to condoms. Sometimes the pitches are direct and sometimes they're delivered with a come-hither smirk. What's the story?

IS THE HEART MAKING PURCHASE DECISIONS OR THE LIBIDO?

Fifty-three percent of people are more likely to buy a product that is advertised using the imagery of love, than one that relies on sexual innuendo.

ARE YOU INSULTED BY MARKETERS USING SEX TO SELL?

One in three adults claim they're offended by ads that use sex to sell. Perhaps surprisingly, considerably more of them are men. Forty-five percent of men versus 24 percent of women turn off to advertising that blatantly uses sex.

WHY ALL THE SEX IN ADS THEN?

Because research has shown that 44 percent of eighteen- to twenty-four-year-olds are more likely to buy clothes if an ad showcasing them uses sexual images. But raw sex doesn't work in all categories. Many more people would be inclined to buy furniture that used images of love than would be motivated by images of sex. And 35 percent say a message of love would make them want to buy appliances, while only 8 percent say sex would help clinch the sale.

DO YOU PAY MORE ATTENTION TO ADS WITH SEXUAL IMAGERY?

A third of people think they're likely to pay more attention to an ad if it contains images of sex. Half of wealthier Americans who disdain love themes in ads respond to sex in ads. And while half of those in casual relationships perk up by sexual content, only 28 percent of those in committed relationships do.

DO YOU SEE THE JIGGLE AND FANTASIZE YOURSELF IN THE SITUATION?

Two-thirds of women say they identify with the women they see in ads and think they're portrayed realistically.

DO YOU THINK THERE'S TOO MUCH SEX ON TV?

Two-thirds of adults think the amount of sexual imagery on TV is becoming obscene. Eighty-three percent want to see 8 P.M. to 9 P.M. become a raunch-free hour. In fact, this so-called family hour has grown almost twice as permissive over the past few years, with one out of seven shows featuring sexual intercourse, either depicted or strongly implied, according to the Henry J. Kaiser Family Foundation. Four years ago it was one in fourteen shows. Two-thirds of all shows from 7 A.M. to 11 P.M. have some sexual content, ranging from sex talk to depictions of sexual behavior. Four years ago Kaiser found the figure was about half that.

DO YOU THINK SEXY CLOTHES MAKE A VICTIM CULPABLE?

A third of men and one in five women feel that ladies who dress revealingly are "asking for" sex.

29

Would You Rather . . .

HAVE MORE ROMANCE, AFFECTION, OR SEX?

If we could notch up only one of these in our relationships, romance wins by a shade. Thirty-one percent of people worldwide opt for it, while one in four weighs in for more affection——the same amount as want to intensify the sex. A fifth would simply like to get in a relationship. While it may not be surprising that the French opt for more sex (36 percent), hold the chopsticks; 55 percent of Chinese also want it! Forty-two percent of Mexicans want to snuggle more, while 44 percent of the Dutch and Spanish yearn for more affection.

HAVE SEX OR ROMANCE IN YOUR LIFE BUT NOT BOTH?

Almost three out of four of us would pick the hearts and flowers although the split is closest in China where 43 percent would opt for a lifetime of sex without romance. Seventy-five percent of Americans, faced with this painful choice, would rather have romance than sex.

HAVE INTERCOURSE WITH YOUR LOVER OR A MEANINGFUL CONVERSATION?

Fluff the couch pillows: more than four out of five women told *Dear Abby* that they would prefer sitting on the sofa to have a heart-to-heart talk than romping in the sheets.

GO OUT WITH FRIENDS OR HAVE SEX?

Sex loses yet again. More than a fifth of folks choose playing with their peers to having sex with their partner. Another 10 percent prefer to either play sports or go shopping. Yet more people would rather have a romantic evening with their partner than a long chat with their closest friend, even with a bag of chips and chocolate thrown in.

HAVE SOMEONE BRAINY OR BUILT?

Brains win, but not by a landslide. Fewer than half of people pick intelligence although it's skewed by gender (60 percent of women versus 34 percent of men). Forty-three percent of men admit that while they're not proud of it, they're more swayed by a good body, whereas only 24 percent of women are. Fourteen percent say they can't be attracted to someone who didn't have both (10 percent of women and 17 percent of men).

HAVE AN HOUR TO YOURSELF OR WITH YOUR LOVER?

More than half of women prefer an hour of luxurious privacy to 60 shared minutes in the bedroom. What would they do with the time? The top pick: shop.

HAVE BIGGER BREASTS OR BIGGER PAYCHECK?

Three out of four women would rather increase the size of their income than the size of their breasts. Men concur.

HAVE THE PRELUDE OR THE ORCHESTRA?

Two-thirds of us enjoy the act itself more than the foreplay leading up to it—with men likelier than women to feel this way.

TALK ABOUT POOR SEXUAL PERFORMANCE OR INFIDELITY?

Which is the worse of two evils? By far, it's infidelity. By a wide margin people would rather discuss disappointing sexual performance than cheating on their partner.

TALK ABOUT SEX WITH YOUR PARENTS OR ASK FOR A LOAN?

They must *really* not want to discuss money because young folks (eighteen to thirty years old) would rather talk to Mom and Dad about their sex lives than discuss their finances—or ask for a little something to tide them over. They're more apt to ask if their girlfriend or boyfriend can stay in their room overnight at their parents' home than respond to inquiries about their monetary situation.

TELL MOM WHY YOU'RE STILL SINGLE OR HAVE A TOOTH PULLED?

While most singles shrug this off as no big deal, for 10 percent the annual holiday chore of explaining why they are not busily producing grandchildren is worse than a painful tooth extraction.

HAVE SPONTANEOUSLY PICKED WILDFLOWERS OR A DOZEN LONG STEMS?

Save your money; some 62 percent of us consider a bouquet of wildflowers plucked from the side of the road far more romantic than beautiful store-bought long-stemmed red roses.

HAVE A CANDLELIT DINNER AT HOME OR AT A FANCY RESTAURANT?

By an almost two to one margin, people find the home dinner more romantic . . . as long as they're not responsible for the cleanup.

BE STRANDED ON AN ISLAND TO TEST YOUR STAMINA OR TAKEN TO A LUXURIOUS RESORT TO TEST YOUR MARITAL FIDELITY?

Perhaps inspired by the so-called reality TV shows that have ambushed America, considerably more people would opt for the fidelity-testing resort over the endurance-testing island.

HAVE MORE SLEEP AND LESS SEX OR MORE SEX AND LESS SLEEP?

Shut-eye squeaks past sex by a hair, but men picked sex over sleep by a landslide.

GIVE UP SEX OR YOUR FAVORITE FOOD?

Perhaps the way to a man's or woman's heart is not through his or her stomach after all. Seventy-seven percent of women would even give up truffles, while one in five would sacrifice sex. Ninety-one percent of men would ditch the food; just 7 percent would forfeit sex. On the other hand, never underestimate the power of food. Given the choice between a great restaurant meal or great sex, 56 percent of women would go gourmet, leaving 44 percent to hit the sheets.

HAVE SEX OR CHOCOLATE?

Men overwhelmingly prefer sex to chocolate, but only a slender majority of women agree. Just 57 percent would rather have sex than eat chocolate versus 85 percent of men. Ten percent of snackers of both sexes would rather eat snacks than make love.

WATCH FOOTBALL OR HAVE SEX?

Pass the pigskin. Three out of four American men claim they'd rather watch a football game featuring a team they support—either at a stadium enjoying the live action or on TV—than have sex with their wives or regular partners.

BUY A BRA THAT'S SEXY OR PRACTICAL?

Sorry, guys, but practicality wins. More than 70 percent of all bras in the U.S. are "workhorses," simple, comfortable, durable, everyday styles instead of lacy numbers.

WEAR A TANK OR TANKINI?

Show some skin: nearly half of people—45 percent of both men and women—consider bikinis the sexiest swimwear around. Thirty percent think tankinis are the more sultry. Least seductive: one-piece styles with 25 percent of the vote.

HEAR LITTLE WHITE LIES OR BRUTAL HONESTY?
Fifty-six percent of us think a little flattery or exaggeration goes a long way in love. Only 44 percent would rather hear the whole truth and nothing but.

GET A GUSHY LETTER OR GLITTERING GEMS?
Eighty-two percent of women say they'd rather get a mushy missive from their guy than diamond earrings.

HAVE INTIMACY OR ORGASM?
For 44 percent it's the closeness that the act confers, while a third are turned on by the eroticism. Sixteen percent say they most enjoy the orgasm itself, while 7 percent savor the conquest.

GET FIRED OR WALK A MILE ON A BEACH IN AN ITSY BITSY, ALL TOO REVEALING BIKINI?
Hide the pink slip: 71 percent would find getting fired more emotionally roiling. But that means a good chunk of us would be undone by the bikini.

LOSE YOUR CELLPHONE OR YOUR WALLET?
Connecting has become more important than paying for it, it seems. Nearly three-quarters of mobile phone owners say they'd rather lose their wallet than their phone.

DATE A GUY WHO SPENDS MORE TIME ON HIS HAIR THAN YOU DO, OR ONE WHO GETS BAD HAIRCUTS?
Forty-four percent would rather go out with a man who spends a lot of time looking in the mirror, while 14 percent would prefer the fellow who doesn't care what he sees there. The rest consider both unacceptable.

WHICH CONCERNS YOU MORE—THE SIZE OF THE NATIONAL DEBT OR THE SIZE OF YOUR PENIS?
Fifty-five percent go with the national debt.

HAVE A LADY WITH SMALL PERFECT BREASTS, LARGE SAGGING ONES, OR LARGE PLASTIC ONES, GUYS?

Half of guys opt for the small and perfect breasts, 15 percent for the buxom but imperfect variety, and 34 percent for large, firm implant stock.

HEAR WOMEN DISCUSS THEIR WEIGHT OR THEIR PERIODS, GUYS?

The most dreaded conversation: menstruation, followed by dieting and weight, men's shortcomings, the listener's specific shortcoming's, and sex in general.

HAVE TICKETS TO A CONCERT OR SHOW OR A HUNDRED-DOLLAR GIFT CERTIFICATE FROM A SWEETHEART?

Four times as many want to be taken out than bought off.

HAVE SCHOOLS TEACH SAFE SEX OR ABSTINENCE?

Two out of three Americans would rather have their local schools teach abstinence than birth control in sex education classes. Westerners are more likely than denizens of other regions to buck the trend and express comfort in teaching safe sex.

RENEW WEDDING VOWS ON A 25TH ANNIVERSARY OR MAKE NEW VOWS?

Despite all those fragrance ads featuring first-time brides, by a three to one margin Americans consider a couple married twenty-five years and renewing their vows to be more romantic than newbies to the marriage game.

HAVE A SAXOPHONE OR VIOLIN CREATE A ROMANTIC ATMOSPHERE?

Neither. The most romantic instrument turns out to be a piano, followed by a saxophone and human voice, while the violin drums up a mere 11 percent of the vote. People are almost equally divided over whether being serenaded in a restaurant is romantic or annoying.

HAVE A QUICKIE OR LONG LANGOROUS LOVEMAKING?

Just 16 percent want to get a move on it and tend to other things.

GO TO YOUR PLACE OR THEIRS?

Fifty-three percent of us would rather make love in our own bedrooms, whereas 47 percent would rather get between the sheets at a hotel room.

GET DIAMONDS OR PEARLS?

Ice is nicer: by a 79 to 21 percent majority.

GO TO A MUSEUM OR A LIBRARY?

Museums are a much sexier venue than libraries by a three to one margin.

HAVE A STORMY NIGHT OR A SUNNY DAY?

Thunder and lightning is the ticket for nearly twice as many people as those who crave clear blue skies for lovemaking.

HAVE PREMATURELY GRAY HAIR OR A SHAVED HEAD, GUYS?

Gray matters. Seventy-one percent find prematurely gray hair (like that of Steve Martin) foxier than a shaved head. Twenty-nine percent think bald—at least on Billy Zane—is beautiful.

DATE A CLEAN-SHAVEN GUY OR ONE WITH A FIVE-O'CLOCK SHADOW?

Stubble is *hot*. Eighty-nine percent of women find the hint of a beard more enticing than a hairless face.

PEOPLE WORE SPANDEX OR CHIFFON?

As for fabrics, three out of four people find the subtle suggestion of what's beneath sheer chiffon more seductive than body-hugging spandex.

WEAR CASHMERE OR SILK?

Sixty-three percent of us prefer cashmere as the fabric we'd like closest to our skin.

SLEEP ON SATIN OR COTTON SHEETS?
Satin may be the fabric of our imaginary sex lives but 73 percent of us prefer to sleep on cotton.

RIDE IN A HORSE-DRAWN CARRIAGE OR A SLEEK LIMO?
Go by coach: almost twice as many people opt for a horse-drawn carriage over a sleek limo.

BE DISCREET OR OUT IN THE OPEN?
Just 15 percent say they get a bigger kick out of doing it in public than kissing behind closed doors.

SIT IN A SAUNA OR STEAM ROOM?
Fifty-four percent of us go for the dry heat.

DISCUSS A SEX FANTASY WITH YOUR PARTNER OR WATCH A HARD-CORE PORN MOVIE?
Talk triumphs: 38 percent of women and 43 percent of men would rather make it personal than watch others go at it on the screen.

HAVE YOUR PARTNER CONCENTRATE ON YOUR GENITALS OR NIPPLES DURING FOREPLAY?
Go for the "G": 37 percent of women and 58 percent of men would rather their partners focus there, while 28 percent of women and 10 percent of men point them to the chest. The neck is more erogenous than the mouth, it seems, for both men and women.

HAVE YOUR CAREER OR YOUR GIRLFRIEND, GUYS?
The girlfriend is more valuable by an almost three to one margin. They also trump buddies, the car, and dog.

SPEND YOUR SATURDAY NIGHT HANGING WITH THE GUYS AT A BAR OR DINING WITH YOUR GIRLFRIEND AT A RESTAURANT, GUYS?
Dinner with the girlfriend edges out yucking it up with the fellows 47 to 40 percent. For another 11 percent the perfect Saturday night is lolling on the sofa watching a big game.

DEAL WITH YOUR MONEY OR YOUR MARRIAGE?

Money issues are more than three times more nettlesome for men than keeping their partners happy.

RECEIVE TICKETS TO THE SUPER BOWL OR TAKE A SUPERMODEL ON A DATE?

Some 53 percent of guys would rather bond with their buddies at the big game than spend a night on the town with a bombshell.

BE WITH PEONIES OR YOUR PARTNER, LADIES?

Twenty-five percent of women would rather spend time in the garden than have sex.

YOUR PARTNER WORE A BRA THAT HOOKS IN THE FRONT OR THE REAR, GUYS?

Sixty percent of men prefer bras that fasten in front.

DATE A GUY WHO'S INEXPERIENCED BUT SMELLS GOOD OR ONE WHO'S GREAT IN BED, BUT SMELLS BAD, LADIES?

There's reason to sweat the small stuff after all: 80 percent of women opt for the fresh air.

TAKE TIME TO TRAVEL, BE WITH FRIENDS, OR ROMANCE YOUR PARTNER?

If they could have more time for just one thing, women around the globe would rather travel (26 percent) than make love (14 percent). They'd even prefer to have some yucks with friends and family (15 percent) than with their lover, it seems.

SHOP OR SEX?

More than half of women would rather shop than make love, but 93 percent of men prefer sex to shopping.

LIVE WITH OR MARRY?

Not surprisingly men would rather have the milk for free than buy the cow, but somewhat surprisingly, women agree. Two out of three women say they'd prefer to live with a man than marry him.

30

What I'd Do for Love

Love requires sacrifice—giving up cigarettes, bachelorhood, etc. How far are you prepared to go?

WOULD YOU HAVE SEX WHEN YOU'RE NOT IN THE MOOD?
Fifty-five percent would have sex even when they didn't feel like it if they thought it would keep the peace or enhance their marriage.

HOW ABOUT TRY SOMETHING SEXUAL THAT YOU CONSIDER UNSAVORY?
Forty-eight percent would give a sexual act or position they'd disdained a shot and 45 percent would watch an X-rated movie with their husbands.

WOULD YOU GO TO A MARRIAGE COUNSELOR?
Four out of five would seek professional help if *their* relationships were floundering.

WOULD YOU RELOCATE IF YOUR PARTNER WERE TRANSFERRED?

Three out of four would pack up and move . . . even if somewhat reluctantly. On the other hand, 54 percent would willingly turn down a job that meant moving if their partners objected.

WOULD YOU QUIT YOUR JOB IF YOUR PARTNER WANTED YOU HOME?

We may bend and yield but we're far less likely to change who we are just to please a partner. Slightly more than one in three women would resign from their jobs if their husbands preferred that they stay at home.

WOULD YOU CHANGE YOUR DRESS STYLE IF YOUR PARTNER ASKED?

Only 35 percent of us would slip into something slinkier—or more conservative as the case may be—to win partner approval. But if he or she made a good case as to why we looked better that way, we're all ears.

WOULD YOU TRY TO SHED SOME POUNDS TO MAKE YOUR FELLA HAPPY?

Even fewer (30 percent) would try to gain or lose weight if they thought they looked fine but their husbands thought otherwise. Take me as I am or not at all, they say.

WOULD YOU PRETEND TO LIKE A GIFT YOUR PARTNER GAVE YOU?

Nearly four in five women acknowledge cooing over a gift they disliked. What was all that fake oohing and aahing about? Fifty-three percent pretended to be thrilled by some item of clothing, 20 percent by jewelry, and 15 percent by chocolate—even if they were on a diet. Fourteen percent professed a keen desire to read the handyman's guide to plumbing—or whatever book he bought.

WOULD YOU TAKE A MALE BIRTH CONTROL PILL, FELLAS?

Four out of ten guys are willing as long as there are no side effects. Twenty-one percent would do it even if it added fifteen pounds to their torso. But 22 percent would spurn it flat out.

WOULD YOU MOVE ACROSS THE COUNTRY TO BE NEAR THE ONE YOU LOVE?
Sixty percent of folks say they would drop everything to join the person they love.

IF YOUR PARTNER ASKED YOU TO HAVE SEX WITH SOMEONE ELSE WHILE HE OR SHE WATCHED, WOULD YOU?
Seventy percent of women are indignant at the suggestion, including 11.5 percent who consider that out-of-left-field request sufficient cause to call it quits. The rest would seriously consider the proposition, being that it would please their mate. A third of men would reject the idea flat out with 6.6 percent of them considering it impetus to break up with the requester. But a third would take the request seriously, and plow ahead on an adventure that may be fun.

WOULD YOU DONATE AN ORGAN TO YOUR PARTNER?
A third of people vow they'd undergo an excruciating bone marrow transplant or donate a kidney for the possibility of saving their partner's life.

DO YOU WANT TO GET MARRIED?
That's why we did it, claim 89 percent of newlyweds. As for the rest, 6 percent said they did it because they were pregnant or had gotten someone pregnant, were lonely, or attracted to their partner's money.